PEOPLE OF
THE WESTERN RANGE
✢

TIME®
LIFE
BOOKS

This volume is one of a series that chronicles the history and culture of the Native Americans. Other books in the series include:

The Cover: Perched proudly astride an Appaloosa horse and clutching a feather fan, young Joslyn Leighton of the Nez Percé displays examples of her tribe's intricate handiwork, including a cape embroidered with flowers and a beaded bag adorned with animal motifs. Horses and equestrian finery have long been prized by many tribes of the western range, from the Nez Percé of the Plateau to the Shoshones of the eastern Basin.

PEOPLE OF
THE WESTERN RANGE

✛

by
THE EDITORS
of
TIME-LIFE BOOKS

ALEXANDRIA, VIRGINIA

Time-Life Books is a division of Time Life Inc.

PRESIDENT and CEO: John M. Fahey Jr.
EDITOR-IN-CHIEF: John L. Papanek

TIME-LIFE BOOKS

MANAGING EDITOR: Roberta Conlan

Director of Design: Michael Hentges
Director of Editorial Operations: Ellen Robling
Director of Photography and Research: John Conrad Weiser
Senior Editors: Russell B. Adams Jr., Dale M. Brown, Janet Cave, Lee Hassig, Robert Somerville, Henry Woodhead
Special Projects Editor: Rita Thievon Mullin
Director of Technology: Eileen Bradley
Library: Louise D. Forstall

PRESIDENT: John D. Hall

Vice President, Director of Marketing: Nancy K. Jones
Vice President, Director of New Product Development: Neil Kagan
Vice President, Book Production: Marjann Caldwell
Production Manager: Marlene Zack
Quality Assurance Manager: Miriam P. Newton

Library of Congress Cataloging in Publication Data
People of the western range/by the editors of Time-Life Books.
    p.   cm.—(The American Indians)
    Includes bibliographical references and index.
    ISBN 0-8094-9725-5
    1. Indians—North America—Great Basin. 2. Indians—North America—Columbia Plateau. I. Time-Life Books. II. Series.
E78.G67P46 1995   94-43685
979'.01—dc20   CIP

THE AMERICAN INDIANS
SERIES EDITOR: Henry Woodhead
Administrative Editor: Loretta Y. Britten

Editorial Staff for *People of the Western Range*
Art Director: Mary Gasperetti
Picture Editor: Jane Coughran
Text Editor: Stephen G. Hyslop
Associate Editor/Research-Writing: Robert Wooldridge
Senior Copyeditor: Ann Lee Bruen
Picture Coordinator: Daryl Beard
Editorial Assistant: Christine Higgins

Special Contributors: Ronald Bailey, Jim Hicks, David S. Thomson, Gerald P. Tyson (text); Elizabeth Schleichert (research-writing); Martha Lee Beckington, Sara Labouisse, Anne Whittle, Jayne Rohrich Wood (research); Barbara L. Klein (index).

Correspondents: Christine Hinze (London), Christina Lieberman (New York), Maria Vincenza Aloisi (Paris). Valuable assistance was also provided by: Caroline Alcock Wood (London), Elizabeth Brown (New York), Carolyn Sackett (Seattle).

CONTENTS

1
A LAND OF GIFTS AND GATHERINGS

2
ALIENS IN THEIR OWN DOMAIN

3
IN DEFENSE OF THE HOMELAND

ESSAYS

FACES ACROSS TIME

SHOSHONE WARRIOR, 1890

RANDY WEST, SHOSHONE, 1988

NEZ PERCÉ WOMAN, C. 1900

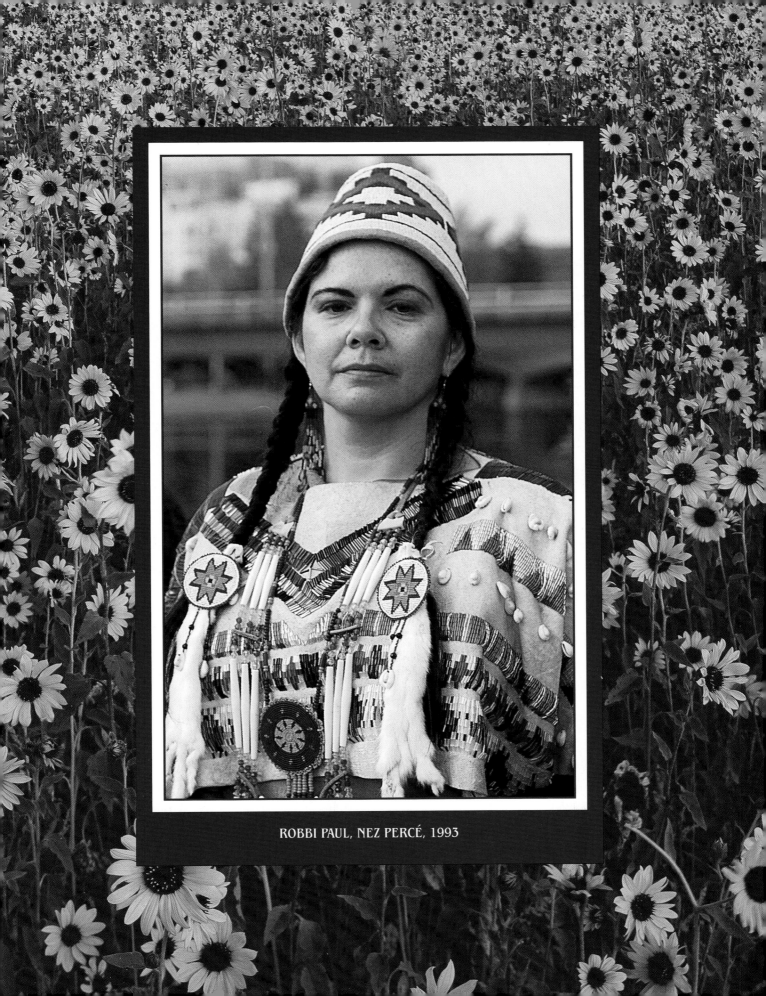

ROBBI PAUL, NEZ PERCÉ, 1993

CHIEF TABBY, UTE, C. 1890

EDDIE BOX, SOUTHERN UTE, 1989

UMATILLA YOUTH, 1910

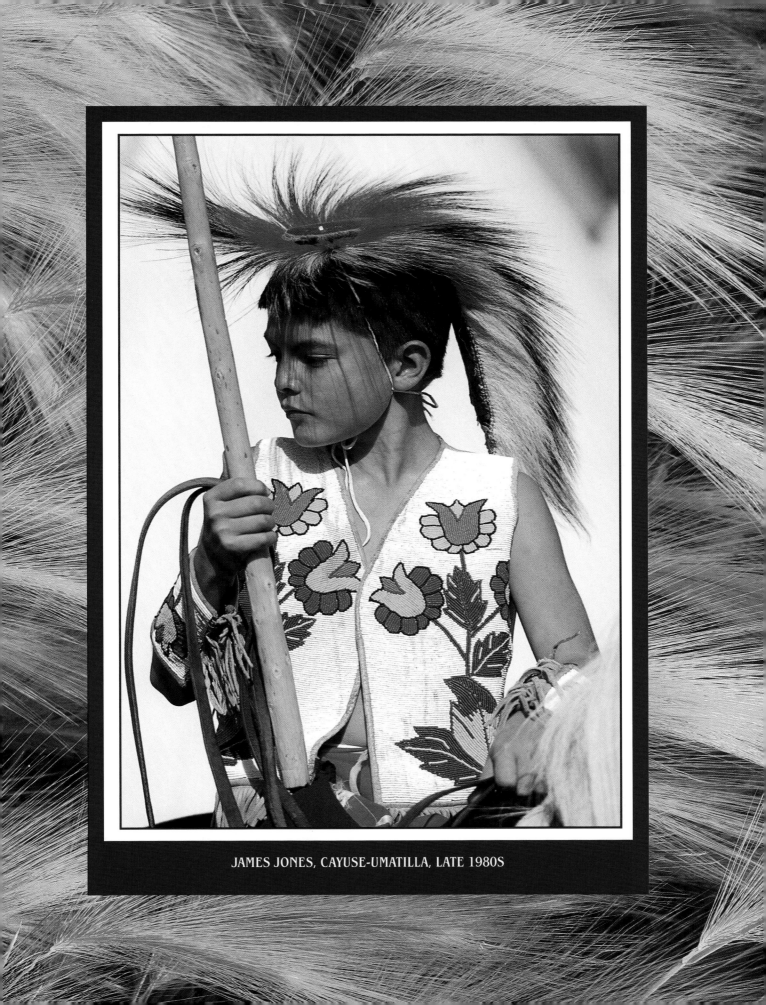

JAMES JONES, CAYUSE-UMATILLA, LATE 1980S

SU-DOHN (OSIER-WILLOW BLOSSOM), PAIUTE, 1924

KATIE FRAZIER, PAIUTE, 1986

1

A LAND OF GIFTS AND GATHERINGS

Firing into the air, hundreds of Indians celebrate the opening of a rendezvous along the Green River in Wyoming in 1837. Goods exchanged at this annual trade fair circulated far and wide. The knife above, with a blade of obsidian from the Yellowstone region near the rendezvous site, was found in Ohio.

Long before white men crossed their lands in pursuit of furs and fortune, Indians of many tribes traveled hundreds of miles each year to trade and mingle with one another in what is now Wyoming, arriving there in the Green River valley in late spring or early summer when the passes were free of snow. They came from throughout the western range—the vast expanse cupped between the Rocky Mountains to the east and the Sierra Nevada and Cascade Range to the west. Some of the visitors would be known to posterity by names of Indian origin, others by European labels. From the Columbia Plateau to the northwest came Cayuses, Umatillas, Nez Percés, and Flatheads, among others. From nearby and from distant reaches of the Great Basin to the southwest came Shoshones, Bannocks, and Utes. The gathering even attracted Crow Indians from the Plains beyond the Continental Divide, due east of the river valley.

The exact location of the get-together may have shifted from year to year, but it most likely occurred near the valley's narrow northern end. There below towering peaks, grassy meadows and leafy cottonwood trees offered a more congenial setting than did the seemingly endless expanses of sagebrush farther south. Later, when whites entered the region, that verdant spot was adopted as a rendezvous point by fur-trapping mountain men, who felt as welcome there as the Indians who had long frequented the place—and still did so to barter and commune with the trappers. "The summer rendezvous was always where there was grass for the animals, and game for the camp," recalled mountain man Joe Meek. "The plains bordered by picturesque mountain ranges, the waving grass, variegated with wild flowers; the clear summer heavens flecked with white clouds that threw soft shadows; the lodges, around which clustered the camp in motley garb and brilliant coloring; gay laughter, and the murmur of soft Indian voices, all made up a most spirited and enchanting picture."

In earlier times, as in the days of the mountain men, such hospitable surroundings accommodated thousands of Indians—men, women, and

children, who arrived with their belongings piled high on their backs or packed onto horses or dog-drawn travois. They came prepared to stay for a while. Bannocks and Shoshones brought the long poles and buffalo hides that would form their tipis, as did Crows visiting from the Plains and various groups from the Plateau who lived within range of buffalo country. Others carried mats of reeds or bark to cover their shelters.

Once they had pitched camp, Indians visited with other bands, talking in signs when language barriers barred spoken communication. Members of different tribes told tales together, hunted together, feasted and danced as one around the campfires, and competed in tests of horsemanship and strength. But the festivities did not long divert them from their central purpose in making the long trek here every year—the exchange of goods.

Indian trading ties in the mountainous West were extensive and long-standing. Spaniards who first encountered the Pueblo peoples in the 16th century found them busily engaged in a trade network that extended up through the Great Basin to the Pacific Northwest. Among the commodities bartered to and fro were items made of polished seashells from the Pacific Coast, gleaming turquoise from the Southwest, and hard black obsidian extruded eons earlier by Great Basin volcanoes.

Those prizes and many others changed hands at the rendezvous. Indians offering goods for barter there either laid them out for display, perhaps on buffalo hides or rush mats spread on the ground, or hauled them about in woven fiber baskets or hide bags, proudly reaching in to pull out samples of their wares when haggling for products offered by others. The profusion of goods was remarkable to behold. Nez Percés and Umatillas arrived with treasures from the Pacific Coast, obtained at the trading center known today as The Dalles, on the Columbia River. Those coastal imports included oils from fish and sea mammals for cooking and cosmetic use; whale bone and seal bone; and ornamental shells, including the tapered, tubular mollusk shells called dentaliums, or tooth shells, which held such enduring appeal that some tribes used them as currency. From their own country, Plateau tribes brought piles of furs, finely woven baskets of various sizes and shapes, and containers of crushed minerals and vegetable matter that were mixed with liquid to make paints.

Crow Indians brought soft, rose-colored pipestone from the heart of the continent for sculpting into pipes; quarried in Minnesota, the stone likely passed through various hands before Crow middlemen acquired it in trade along the Missouri. The Crows also brought prized items from their own land—including buffalo robes and beads carved from buffalo bone—

Beyond a placid stream, Wyoming's Wind River mountains soar skyward in the ancestral homeland of the Eastern Shoshones. Indians long traveled westward through passes in this range to reach the annual gathering along the Green River.

and in later years, European-made wares such as metal axes. Utes of the southern Basin offered alluring items obtained from the Spaniards or the Spanish-influenced Pueblo Indians, including shiny knife blades, mirrors, and brightly colored glass beads.

From throughout the Basin came buckskins, antelope and elk hides, women's dresses made from skins, rabbit-fur blankets, tools of obsidian and other stone, powerful bows of wood laminated with horn for extra strength and resilience, and arrows fletched with prized eagle feathers. Indians from around the western range offered well-preserved foodstuffs, including acorn and pine nut meal, smoked salmon and dried crickets, starchy bitterroot, and the flavorful bulbs of camas lilies. Basin Indians also brought wild tobacco, the prime plants being those that grew in areas they had purposely burned over to improve the quality of the leaf.

Goods exchanged at the rendezvous found their way to the far ends of the continent and beyond. The oils that Nez Percé traders packed in from Oregon were carried by Utes to the pueblos of the Southwest and by Crows to their Mandan and Arikara trading partners along the Missouri River. Minnesota pipestone ended up in the hands of Indians on the Northwest Coast, while furs from the Plateau found their way to the storerooms of Spanish merchants in Mexico, who then shipped some of the hides to Europe.

But of all the items offered at the rendezvous, none were more in demand or had a greater effect on the lives of the Indians than horses. Utes were the first in the region to acquire those animals. By the mid-1600s, they were buying or stealing horses from the Spaniards or from tribes in contact with them. Profiting from their newfound mobility, the Utes began making mounted expeditions to the Plains in pursuit of buffalo. Soon they were driving herds of horses north to the rendezvous, which became by far the biggest horse market in the region. The animals were coveted by most groups of the region who had pastures to support sizable herds. Some tribes on the Plateau—notably the Coeur d'Alene, Palouse, Nez Percé, and Cayuse—gained expertise in breeding and training horses and offered stiff competition to the Utes as traders. (In time, the term *cayuse* became common western parlance for pony, while the Palouse gave their name to the Appaloosa horse, although the Nez Percé may well have had a hand in developing that spotted breed.)

Some other tribes of the western range that lacked good grazing areas or good reason to venture far from home on horseback acquired few if any mounts and were affected only indirectly by the profound cultural changes the animal wrought. Once horses reached the rendezvous, how-

Two Indians—one carrying a fishnet attached to a pole and the other a basket to haul away the catch—prepare to draw salmon from the gorge at The Dalles, where the Columbia River cuts down from the Plateau to the Pacific Coast. For ages, the place was both a favorite fishing spot and a trading junction for tribes from the coast and the interior. These comb fragments, carved of bone, were found at The Dalles, where they were probably offered in trade.

ever, they became its trademark. In the early 1800s, when Indians gathered with mountain men along the Green River, the two sides found common ground in their love for horses and for all the ceremony attending them—from races and displays of trick riding to mock attacks by mounted warriors and mountain men on visitors approaching the get-together for the first time. One such newcomer, William Gray, told of being accosted with others en route to the rendezvous. "Two hours before we reached camp," he recalled, "the whole caravan was alarmed by the arrival of some 10 Indians and four or five white men, whose dress and appearance could scarcely be distinguished from that of the Indians. As they came in sight over the hills, they all gave a yell, such as hunters and Indians only can give." The raucous reception party fired their guns in the air and circled the caravan, spurring their mounts to wild leaps and turns. It was difficult to tell which was crazier, Gray observed, "the horse or the rider."

Such boisterous greetings were a way for Indians—and for mountain men who adopted many of their ways—to signal that this was still Indian country and that visitors would have to act accordingly. Soon, however, whites would arrive on the western range in strength and openly defy the customs and privileges of native peoples. That onslaught would tear at the very roots of tribal cultures. At risk were age-old Indian traditions that were delicately attuned to the rhythms of the land—its recurring hardships and persistent rewards, its long seasons of deprivation and startling bursts of generosity, its desolate trails and delightful meeting places.

The Indians of the western range have long made the most of its varied terrain. In broad terms, the Great Basin to the south consists of dry and open country, while the Columbia Plateau to the north is graced with more moisture and dominated by forested slopes and grassy valleys. Yet that distinction can be deceptive. Parts of the Plateau, notably the lowlands of central Washington and neighboring Oregon, remain arid and unyielding through much of the year, while mountainous areas of the Basin such as the Humboldt Range of Nevada and the Wasatch Range of Utah harbor extensive forests and deep winter snowpacks that feed waterways vital to the area's plant and animal life. Indeed, much of the Basin is creased with ridges that draw precious moisture from the fleeting storm clouds and support groves of nut-bearing piñon trees and other rich food sources.

As its name implies, the Basin forms a vast undulating sink, enclosed within higher ground. At its margins, two rivers—the Colorado and the Snake—cut through the terrain, funneling water toward the Gulf of California and the Columbia River estuary, respectively. Yet the Basin proper has no outlet to the sea. Its few permanent rivers and many seasonal streams empty into lakes and marshes that, along with the region's wooded mountaintops, have done much to sustain life in an otherwise inhospitable environment.

The Basin was once a watery place. In the aftermath of the latest Ice Age, melting glaciers left behind huge lakes that fostered rain and snowfall in surrounding areas. Over thousands of years, however, the climate grew warmer and drier, and the lakes shriveled. Evaporation ultimately reduced the Basin's largest body of water, known today as the Great Salt Lake, to a fraction of its original area and rendered it highly saline. Some smaller lakes in the region remained fresh, thanks to runoff from the mountains. Once the Basin had lost its vast reservoirs of antiquity and grown dependent on moisture flowing from the Pacific, however, the steep rain shield of the Sierras to the west left much of the area forbiddingly dry.

Native peoples first migrated onto the Basin about 10,000 years ago, while the environment was in transition. For some time, the climate remained cooler and wetter than it is today, but the Basin dwellers ultimately had to adapt to severely arid conditions. They did so by remaining highly mobile—trekking up and down the ridges and back and forth across the lowlands from marshes to fields of wild grain and other seasonal foraging stops. Although they sometimes hunted antelope and mountain goats, they were less likely to feast on large animals than on jack rabbits,

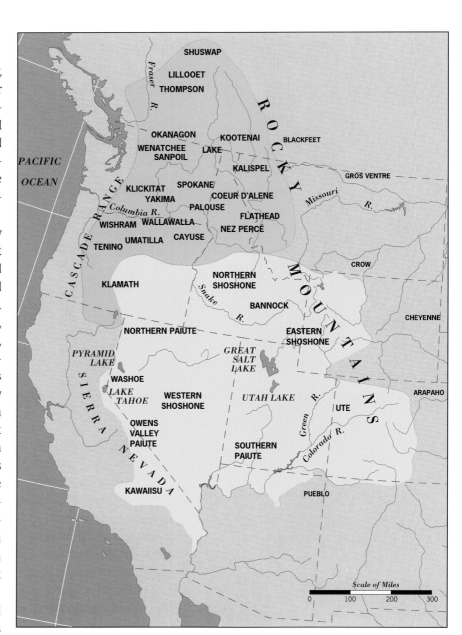

Tribes of the western range occupied the rugged terrain between the Continental Divide and the Cascades and Sierras. Among those inhabiting the Great Basin were Paiutes, Shoshones, Bannocks, and Utes. The Columbia Plateau to the north was home to sundry peoples, including buffalo hunters such as the Nez Percés and Flatheads, who made mounted forays onto the Plains, as did the Utes and Shoshones of the eastern Basin.

This six-inch-high clay image of a woman was among many mysterious figures crafted by Indians of the ancient Fremont culture that flourished in the Basin before Europeans arrived in the New World.

field mice, snakes, and insects. Survival depended on dispersing into small groups, often single families. Even hospitable parts of the Basin supported an average of only one person per five square miles, while the less inviting areas sustained one person per 50 square miles, at best.

Yet the early Basin dwellers were not without assets or devices, as evidenced by ancient artifacts found stored in a cave in northern Nevada, near a marshy area harboring birds and plant life, especially a reed known as tule. Like Indians frequenting such spots in recent times, the people here ate the roots and seeds of the tule and used the plant fiber to fashion ropes, shoes, garments, baskets, and duck decoys. They also left behind bows and arrows that have been dated to approximately AD 500, shortly before the weapon was adopted by Indians of the eastern woodlands. About that same time, another group arrived in the Basin and began practicing agriculture. For eight centuries, they raised corn at their pueblolike settlements of adobe and stone in Utah, western Colorado, and eastern Nevada. Their communities and way of life, known as the Fremont culture, vanished by the 14th century, perhaps because of prolonged drought.

By then, a fresh migratory wave had swept across the Basin, consisting of hunter-gatherers who arrived from the south sometime before AD 1000. Almost all of those newcomers were Numic speakers—members of the northern branch of the vast Uto-Aztecan language family whose range extended deep into Mexico. Only one Basin people spoke a completely different tongue: the Washoe of the Lake Tahoe area, who belonged to the same Hokan language family as the Pomo and other tribal groups of coastal California.

As the Numic speakers spread out across the region, they formed linguistically distinct tribal groups, whose bonds were reinforced by the periodic gatherings of families that spent much of the year foraging on their own. In winter, for example, dozens of families linked by kinship or long association typically camped together as a band. In other seasons, neighboring bands sometimes convened for weeks on end at lakes, marshes, piñon groves, and other places that were especially rich in food resources. Such meetings and the ceremonies attending them lent a loose tribal identity to people within certain zones. The area from southeastern Oregon down through western Nevada was home to the Northern Paiutes, whose various bands spoke mutually intelligible dialects and shared many customs. Another group speaking a related language—known today as the Owens Valley Paiutes—occupied a narrow zone along the Owens River in eastern California. Distinct from them were the Southern Paiutes, whose bands ranged from the lower California-Nevada border area through southwestern Utah and sometimes gathered at hospitable places to harvest, hunt, trade, and celebrate. Despite their name, the Southern Paiutes were closer linguistically to the Utes, of Utah and Colorado, and to the Kawaiisu—a small tribal group living in southern California near the Nevada border—than they were to the Northern and Owens Valley Paiutes.

The Shoshones, for their part, subdivided into three branches—Western, Eastern, and Northern, the last of which became associated with a neighboring group of Paiutes called Bannocks. In early times, before the advent of the horse, such broad distinctions meant little to the various Shoshone bands, which were commonly identified by their main sources of food. Those relying largely on the bighorn sheep that roamed the mountainsides, for example, were called "sheep eaters." Despite variations in dialect, all Shoshones could understand one another. And originally they all pursued a similar routine, traveling widely on foot in small numbers and convening in larger groups now and then like the Paiutes.

After the arrival of horses, however, the regional distinctions between Shoshones grew sharper. The arid domain of the Western Shoshones, from northwestern Utah through central Nevada, offered poor browsing for horses, and bands there continued to travel on foot and pursue the old subsistence activities. They were sometimes called Shoshoko—meaning Walkers, or Diggers, for the pointed sticks they used to dig wild edible roots from the earth, a technique shared by many peoples of the western range. Although some early white observers disparaged such Diggers as primitives, they were in fact highly resourceful, both in their careful exploitation of wild growth and in their use of ingenious hunting methods like the grasshopper drive, which forced insects spread over several acres into one small pit, to be crushed and dried for future consumption.

The Northern Shoshones and Bannocks in and around the lower part of Idaho inhabited a country that was better watered and more congenial for horses. As a result, many bands there acquired herds of ponies and rode in pursuit of the bison that grazed in modest numbers west of the Continental Divide and in great multitudes on the Plains to the east. For most Northern Shoshones and Bannocks, buffalo hunting remained a supplement to traditional pursuits such as fishing or foraging for camas bulbs. For the Eastern Shoshones in neighboring Wyoming, however, the fine horse pastures along the Green River and its tributaries and the proximity of the Plains made the pursuit of bison their supreme activity. They became known, in fact, as "buffalo eaters" and evolved many cultural

A low sun gilds the valley floor beneath the snowcapped peaks of the Wassuk Range in western Nevada. Basin dwellers used the desert brush to cover the pole frameworks of wickiups like the one built to shelter this family of Bannocks (inset), pictured in 1872.

traits characteristic of Plains tribes. Leaders of their various bands, for example, would meet in council, where they planned hunts and other communal activities and appointed chiefs who exercised wide influence.

No tribal group in the Basin was more affected by the horse than the
Utes. Consisting of a dozen or so bands that lived in the grassy mountain
valleys from central Utah through western Colorado, the Utes spoke related dialects and often cooperated when hunting or making war. Horses
helped them immeasurably in both pursuits, for they not only ranged far
out onto the Plains in pursuit of buffalo but also raided westward into
Nevada and claimed captives from unmounted bands of Shoshones and
Paiutes, some of whom were sold as slaves to Spanish colonists in the

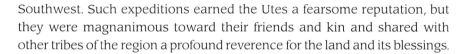
Pictured at a recent Shoshone-Bannock festival in Idaho, horsemen Randy West (far left and below) and Vincent Bono (near left) wear traditional tribal garb. Shoshones and Bannocks adopted such finery in the 18th century after acquiring horses.

Southwest. Such expeditions earned the Utes a fearsome reputation, but they were magnanimous toward their friends and kin and shared with other tribes of the region a profound reverence for the land and its blessings.

Compared to the Basin, the Columbia Plateau afforded native peoples a more generous environment, with certain notable exceptions. The Cascades, while not as steep as the highest of the Sierras, blocked large amounts of moisture from the Pacific and kept the plains east of the mountains parched through the summer. Yet the frequency and intensity of storms moving in from the Northwest Coast, particularly in winter, ensured that much of the Plateau would receive ample precipitation, with the greatest amounts falling in the mountains extending from eastern Washington through western Montana and the neighboring area of British Columbia. Generous runoff from that high ground fed the mighty Columbia River and its many tributaries and made the Plateau as a whole an inviting country indeed. Each year at predictable times, different species of salmon choked the streams in runs so thick that they could virtually be scooped from the water. Sturgeon, trout, and other fish also offered themselves for the taking. Along the rivers, the evergreen forests often teemed with deer and elk, while antelope and rabbits abounded in the high plains and edible roots proliferated in the valleys.

People began to camp along the Columbia River to fish there roughly 11,000 years ago, or not long after the glacial ice had retreated from the area. There was much movement of bands to and fro in early times. But as early as 8,000 years ago, one resourceful group had ensconced itself on the Columbia Plateau for good. Those were members of the Sahaptin language family, whose tribal descendants include the Klickitat, Umatilla, Yakima, Palouse, Cayuse, Wallawalla, and Nez Percé (so called by French traders because some of them shared in the widespread native practice of piercing the nose for ornamental purposes). At the time whites came in contact with them, Sahaptin-speaking tribes occupied a broad band across the southern part of the Plateau, from just east of the Cascades to the Idaho-Montana border.

The ancestors of tribespeople belonging to another major language family, the Salish, arrived in the area some 3,500 years ago and settled to the north and east of the Sahaptin speakers. Salish tribes inhabiting the Plateau in British Columbia at the time of European contact included the Shuswap, Lillooet, Okanagon, Lake, and Thompson. Farther south in what is now American territory dwelt such Salish speakers as the Sanpoil, Kalispel, Spokane, Coeur d'Alene, and Flatheads (called that despite their conventional appearance because they did not elongate the heads of their infants by binding the skull as did Salish peoples on the Northwest Coast). Salish tongues varied greatly and could sound strange to foreign ears. The journal kept by the American explorers Meriwether Lewis and William Clark, who traversed the homeland of the Flatheads in western Montana in 1805, compared their speech to "the clucking of a fowl, or the noise of a parrot." The vocal quirks of English speakers must have seemed equally bizarre to the Indians.

A few other tribes on the Plateau belonged to smaller language groups or occupied a linguistic niche of their own, as did the Kootenai, who lived northwest of the Flatheads. The Wishram, who dwelt along the Columbia River near The Dalles and figured prominently in the intertribal commerce there, spoke Chinook, the language of their coastal trading partners. (A distinct pidgin language, known as Chinook Jargon, evolved from the dealings of the Chinook with Europeans and with other tribes of the lower Columbia.) Overall, the Plateau was one of North America's most diverse regions tribally, embracing more than two dozen different peoples.

Like the Basin dwellers, the Plateau Indians spent much of the year on the move, fishing, hunting, and harvesting wild growth according to an ancient agenda that was sometimes amended by nature's whims—a late salmon run caused by fluctuations in Pacific currents, perhaps, or an early summer berry harvest occasioned by a premature spring. During the warm months, Plateau Indians generally traveled in families or in small groups. Come winter, they convened in villages of up to a few hundred people, settling into their lodges for a season of domestic chores and communal festivities. People from nearby villages often came together for trade, ceremonies, and courtship, all of which promoted tribal bonds.

Beyond this basic pattern, the character of Plateau life was powerfully shaped by location. Several tribes living along the western edge of the Plateau, for instance, became involved in a bustling slave trade with neighboring coastal Indians, whose wealthy chiefs sought captives from the interior to perform menial tasks and enhance the prestige of their households. The Klamath Indians of south-central Oregon formed raiding parties and ventured down into California and out onto the Basin to corral slaves and other booty. The hapless victims were then traded to Chinook

Leaders of Oregon's Umatillas sit proudly on horseback in the front rank, flanked by women of the tribe, in a photograph taken about 1900. Here as elsewhere on the Plateau, the women took to riding and regalia as enthusiastically as the men did.

middlemen, who delivered them into captivity on the coast. Farther north, the Thompson and Lillooet Indians were also energetic slave raiders and dealers, ranging up into the Canadian interior and preying on Athapaskan peoples. Other western Plateau tribes, such as the Klickitat and Yakima, had no likely targets within reach and refrained from slave raiding.

Tribes at the eastern edge of the Plateau, for their part, looked increasingly to the Plains for their livelihood once they acquired horses. Initially, groups such as the Nez Percé, Kootenai, and Flatheads lived much as tribes to their west did, hunting and gathering when the opportunity arose and relying heavily on runs of salmon up the region's rivers. But the advent of the horse about 1700 gave eastern tribes ready access to the Plains and a meaty new staple: the buffalo.

According to a tale told by the Flatheads, they were the first on the

Chief Moses—a leader of Washington's small Columbia tribe in the 1800s—shows off the elegant trappings of his mount, including a splendid horse mask (inset) and other gear similar in design to the surrounding articles, crafted by Plateau Indians.

LEATHER SADDLE WITH BEADED ADORNMENT

BEADED MARTINGALE, OR HORSE COLLAR

HORSE'S HEADBAND WITH QUILLWORK

The black hands on Chief Moses's horse mask—worn in ceremonies and in battle as a protective charm—commemorate a coup Moses performed as a boy when he killed a Blackfeet warrior. The horns on the mask, evoking the power of the buffalo, are made of bison tails; the ruffle consists of sacred eagle feathers.

Plateau to acquire horses. Long before whites arrived, it was said, a bold party of Flatheads ventured south to avenge a surprise attack by some normally friendly Shoshones. They found the Shoshone camp poorly guarded, and one eager Flathead urged an immediate attack. But the chief of the party spotted something intriguing that demanded further scouting—"a herd of hobbled animals, the like of which they had never seen before." The Flatheads spied for days on the strange beasts and their keepers, some of whom amazed the scouts by climbing atop the animals and riding off. Then while most of the Shoshones were away, the Flatheads pounced, killing the men left on guard and stealing the horses. Still wary of the animals, they headed home on foot, driving the horses between them. Finally, a warrior plucked up the courage to mount one of the ponies—only to come tumbling off when it broke into a trot. His daring inspired others, however, and before long many Flatheads had learned to ride horses and care for them. The men who had stolen those first ones, it was said, proudly "notched their coup sticks and were always given great honor."

As this story suggests, the adoption of the horse had an impact that went beyond the search for subsistence to the pursuit of honor and prestige. Even as the horse enabled tribes of the eastern Plateau to make lengthy forays onto the Plains in pursuit of buffalo, it brought them into fierce competition with tribes already ensconced there—notably the powerful Blackfeet, who deeply resented intrusions on their splendid buffalo range just east of the Rockies. "They have always retained a most inveterate hostility to the Flatheads, against whom they wage a continual warfare," reported a fur trapper named Zenas Leonard in 1831. He added that the Blackfeet, who acquired guns through trade well before tribes on the Plateau did, had come close on occasion to "exterminating" the Flatheads. Such was the hostility they and their Plateau neighbors faced that Nez Percé war chiefs reportedly organized intertribal parties of more than 1,000 Indians to stalk the bison and cope with the Blackfeet.

When Plateau warriors succeeded against their rivals, they claimed captives, who were often treated harshly but seldom if ever sold as slaves. The Flatheads, for instance, usually killed male battle captives before returning home because they knew that such men would only try to escape. A few captive warriors might be escorted back to a Flathead village, but only to show them off and let tribespeople vent their sorrow and anger on the prisoners before they were killed. Captured women, on the other hand, were usually spared and incorporated into the tribe. A female prisoner might become the prize of the warrior who captured her, in which capacity she was expected to relieve his wife of drudgery. Any children the man fathered by the captive were accepted as family, although such offspring ranked a step below the wife's own.

Compared to the tribes at either end of the Plateau, those in the central area led a relatively tranquil existence. Alexander Ross, a fur company clerk who traveled across the central Plateau in the early 19th century, noted that the Okanagons he encountered there went into battle only rarely and were quick to embrace the small number of "slaves," or captives, they took. "War not being their trade," he wrote, "there are but few slaves among them, and these few are adopted as children and treated in all respects as members of the family."

Okanagons avoided costly conflicts by staying relatively close to home. But like most other groups across the Plateau, they too acquired the horse, adopting the animal as freely and enthusiastically as they did their captives. Indeed, the horse became central to Plateau culture—and remained so long after tribes there were confined to reservations. Alexander Ross's tribute to the equestrian skill of the typical Okanagon applied equally well to others in the region: "He passes over hill and dale, rock and ravine, at full speed; so that good roads or bad roads, rugged or smooth, all is alike to him. Nor is the fair sex less dexterous in managing the horse; a woman with one child on her back and another in her arms will course the fleetest steed over the most rugged and perilous country."

Throughout the western range, tribes pursued a seasonal round that emphasized mobility—with or without the horse—and the timely exploitation of nature's fleeting gifts. Every chance within reach had to be seized without delay because all that was not consumed or preserved would spoil, and the next hoped-for opportunity might not materialize. A fishing stream could run dry, a blight could destroy a berry crop, or the bison might not appear where they had in years past.

The annual pursuit of sustenance began in the hungry days of early spring. Except on the western edge of the Plateau, where the Pacific moderated the climate, winter was often severe and left tribes with little in reserve. In the Great Basin, the seeds and dried fish and meat that had been stored away for winter were often used up before the cold relented. No new plant growth had appeared yet, and game was scarce. Some of the elderly and frail people died during these bitter weeks.

As spring gradually brought the earth to life, eager hands were quick

JOHNSON-Ute, Chief,

Chief Johnson of the Utes holds a pole that is adorned with an enemy scalp taken as a trophy—a practice shared by some Shoshones and by many Plains tribes the Utes encountered in their ventures on horseback. The proud warrior tradition of the Utes made them formidable opponents of those Indians or whites who antagonized them.

to find tender new grasses and bulbs. Lucky foragers sometimes came across young leaves of wild lettuce and ate them on the spot. Many bands broke camp and trekked to one of the Basin's lakes or marshes, where they harvested edible cattail roots and shoots, collected duck eggs, and used decoys to lure migrating waterfowl into snares or close enough to be shot with arrows. Northern Paiutes made realistic canvasback duck decoys by placing whole duck skins over molded bundles of reeds. Sometimes, hunters immersed themselves in the water and moved the decoys about to make them appear even more lifelike. In late spring, various Basin peoples pursued waterfowl in a way unique to that season, when the young birds were still too immature to fly and the adults were temporarily grounded because they were molting. Indians in rafts made from bundles of tule herded the flightless waterfowl ashore, where they were easily taken.

Among the Washoes, young men and women left their parents and younger siblings in their camps amid the Sierra foothills and climbed to Lake Tahoe. There, more than 6,000 feet above sea level, the water was still ice-cold in April and the shores snow covered. The youngsters caught white-fish with harpoons, wrapped themselves in rabbit-skin blankets at night, and danced and courted with abandon, free from parental supervision. Then they proudly returned to their villages, bearing loads of dried white-fish that would give the hungry adults and children who had stayed home the strength to make their own treks to the lake. By June the whole Washoe tribe was there, waiting for the spawning trout and other fish to enter the lake's tributary streams. According to tradition, Washoe men would learn in dreams when the fish were ready to appear and would alert

other members of the tribe. While waiting, the Washoes danced, sang, and delighted in the instructive tales of tribal elders. When the runs began, people scooped out the fish by the basketful.

Northern Paiutes reaped a similar bounty of spawning fish around Pyramid Lake in northwestern Nevada, while Northern Shoshones and Bannocks used harpoons, weirs, seines, and basket traps to draw spawning salmon from the Snake River in southern Idaho. Utes used barbed arrows attached to long lines to shoot fish and pull them from Utah Lake; some other Basin dwellers netted tiny hatchlings from desert streams swollen with the runoff of melting mountain snows. Women cleaned the fish and hung them for drying as quickly as men could haul them out.

Meanwhile, many native peoples of the Plateau were engrossed in a

Indians net fish at Celilo Falls near The Dalles in 1899. One tribesman said that the salmon swarming up this stretch of the Columbia "were so thick that a spear thrown blindly would usually hit a 20-pound fish."

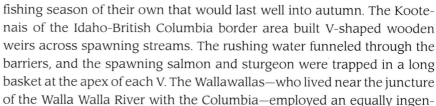

fishing season of their own that would last well into autumn. The Kootenais of the Idaho-British Columbia border area built V-shaped wooden weirs across spawning streams. The rushing water funneled through the barriers, and the spawning salmon and sturgeon were trapped in a long basket at the apex of each V. The Wallawallas—who lived near the juncture of the Walla Walla River with the Columbia—employed an equally ingenious weir, made up of weighted curtains of woven willow mesh that were lowered in pairs across a stream so that crowds of fish became trapped between them.

A young Wishram woman, pictured in 1909, processes dried fish in traditional fashion by pounding it in a stone pestle with a maple-wood mortar. The resulting meal could easily be transported or stored for later use—sometimes with berries mixed in for flavor.

As the spring progressed, many Indians across the western range also spent part of their time hunting—although for most Basin tribes, game remained a mere supplement to a diet of plants, fish, and fowl. For the horseless Western Shoshones, one of the most profitable hunting techniques was the communal antelope drive, held only if enough of the animals were spotted in the vicinity to justify it. Crucial to the undertaking was the leadership of an antelope shaman, an individual who combined a canny knowledge of the prey with a reputation for spiritual empathy with the animals.

Under the shaman's direction, the Shoshones laid out an antelope trap similar to those used by some Plains Indians to drive buffalo—a V-shaped runway, defined by piles of brush and rocks interspersed with men. Next, hunters—sometimes disguised with antelope skins and antlers—crept up on the herd quietly, then began shouting and waving their arms to drive the animals into the open mouth of the V. As the antelopes hurried through the funnel, the Indians at either side prevented their escape and shooed them toward a brush-enclosed corral at the end. There stood the shaman, performing what his followers considered the most important task of the drive. Using powers acquired through rituals and dreams, he charmed the souls of the antelopes and compelled them to enter the pen. Then the corral was closed off, and hunters with bows and arrows made the kill. The hunt concluded with a joyous feast.

Other Basin tribes used similar techniques. Utes employed the same kind of V-shaped drive to funnel antelopes over a cliff edge hidden by brush, below which hunters waited to dispatch any surviving animals. The rugged Ute homeland, riven with canyons and defiles, offered many opportunities for such antelope jumps. But any successful drive was likely to

be the last one in that area for some time. Antelope were not plentiful in the Basin, and the local stock often had to replenish itself for several years—perhaps as long as a decade—before another hunt was warranted.

Plateau tribes used communal drives as well to hunt deer and elk. Kalispel hunters sometimes formed a vast circle some miles in circumference around a scattered, browsing herd of elk or deer, then gradually tightened the ring like a noose before dispatching the animals at close quarters with spears and arrows. The Nez Percés occasionally drove herds of deer or elk into large rivers, then targeted the floundering animals from canoes or from horseback. Some Kootenai bands had a special deer-hunting chief whose role was much like that of the antelope shaman.

In the Basin, fish and game became less available as summer progressed, and more attention was devoted to gathering edible plants. Most people left the dry desert floor and scrambled up the hillsides in search of bulbs and roots, currants and wild onions, gooseberries and thornbush

A Coeur d'Alene hunter armed with a Winchester Model 1896 rides home with a child and puppy for passengers and a mule deer for his larder. The introduction of horses and firearms enabled Plateau Indians to spend less time foraging for small rewards and more time pursuing large game.

berries, and various seeds and wild grains. Much of the harvest required considerable processing before it could be eaten. Wild grains, for instance, had to be winnowed in baskets to separate the unwanted husks from the kernels, which were then ground on stone slabs and preserved as meal or in the form of cakes. Even leafy plants such as wild spinach required treatment in the form of a long soaking to leach away the bitter juices.

On the Plateau, men continued hunting and fishing throughout the summer, while women concentrated on gathering and processing plants. Using sharp, lightweight digging tools made of fire-hardened wood and antler, they unearthed camas bulbs, bitterroot, wild carrots, and other edible roots, drying some in the sun and baking others to prepare them for storage. They preserved such roots as well as many different kinds of berries in tightly coiled baskets, which were sometimes buried in holes dug into dry hillsides and lined with grass. In the winter, women would boil up food from the caches with chunks of meat and handfuls of seasoning, such as pine moss—a black lichen collected from the tree trunks in midsummer. Often the cooking was done in watertight baskets by dropping heated stones into the liquid.

Some of the plants were hard to digest if eaten alone or in excess. A pioneering white missionary who sampled camas bulbs declared that they tasted when cooked like a pleasant blend of chestnuts and prunes, but produced "very disagreeable effects for those who do not like strong odors or the sound that accompanies them." Hungry members of the Lewis and Clark expedition who hastily consumed large amounts of camas that they obtained from the Nez Percés suffered more serious consequences, including diarrhea and vomiting. Later they learned that camas was easier on the stomach if eaten with wild onions or fennel.

Flathead women hang strips of meat on a rack for drying in the sun. In damp weather, the meat would be covered and a fire kindled beneath the rack to continue the drying process. Such techniques were long used to preserve the game that men of the tribe garnered during lengthy hunting expeditions.

Dazzling summer displays of blue camas lilies have long been the cue for the annual harvest of the starchy camas bulbs, once the Plateau's second most important food source after salmon.

A Wanapum woman uses a traditional willow digging stick with an antler handle, like the one at right, to pry camas bulbs from the damp soil near Priest Rapids, Washington.

Throughout the western range, Indians varied their diet with local treats. Washoes picked wild strawberries near Lake Tahoe and ate them straight from the vine or crushed them to form a beverage. People camping near forested areas feasted on gobs of sweet sugar pine sap taken directly from the trees. Others collected cattail seeds before they sprouted in the fall and reduced them to a rich brown paste by roasting the seeds inside a protective covering of leaves. Tribes across the region also harvested scores of plants for the treatment of various ailments, gathering Canadian violet for lung trouble, wild geranium for ulcers, snowberries for the pains of childbirth, and skullcap—a kind of mint—for heart problems.

By far the most important part of the annual round for most Basin dwellers was the early autumn pine nut harvest, referred to by the Washoe as Gumbsabai, or the Big Time. It was a big time, indeed, not only for the amount of food gathered but also for the chance it gave otherwise scattered family groups to socialize and celebrate. This was an opportunity for elders to meet in council, for youngsters to fall in love, and for people of all ages to thank the bountiful spirits. Various groups of Paiutes and Shoshones performed Round Dances to celebrate the harvest that kept their communities intact. For Washoes, the fall ceremony was the culmination of a ritual that began earlier in the year when people buried branches laden with young pine cones by a stream and prayed and danced for a good piñon crop. A ritual leader consulted with spirits in his dreams as to the timing of the harvest, then sent out a messenger with a rawhide thong tied into knots that denoted the number of days before the Big Time. The messenger would carry this string calendar from camp to camp and announce the coming assembly, untying one knot each day.

On the appointed date, Washoes gathered near pine nut groves their ancestors had harvested for centuries and embarked on four days of labor, prayers, and celebration—four being a sacred number to them as it was to many other tribes. Each day the men went out to hunt, while the women ritually bathed themselves before gathering pine nuts. Later in the day, there were races and gambling, as well as prayers and dancing. The dancers often carried piñon-gathering tools—long hooked poles for shaking down the pine cones and baskets for holding the harvest—in the hope that those implements would absorb the blessings summoned by the prayers and songs. The leader who had called the group together fasted during the four days, consuming only small portions of cooked pine nuts and cold water while he prayed for a rich harvest.

After the four days, elders gave to each family a share of the pine nuts

Camas bulbs collected in baskets like the one above were baked slowly in covered pits or mashed and then dried in the sun for storage.

collected by the women and the game taken by the men. No family was to eat its own portion, however. After preparing the food, each family gave its share to another as a gesture of hospitality, receiving a portion in turn. As the meal began, elders prayed over the food and encouraged the people to be peaceful and charitable. After the ceremony, entire families set out for the groves and began the real pine nut harvest, which often lasted for weeks.

Once the pine cones were gathered, they were usually roasted to open the bracts that enclosed the seeds. Some harvesters then stored the cones in covered pits for later processing; others stored the seeds after beating them from the cones. Later, people would shell the seeds as needed by parching them in a tray, cracking them between stones, and winnowing out the hulls. The nuts were then eaten whole or ground into a meal, which was mixed with water and consumed as mush. In recent times, parents have been known to satisfy their children's yen for ice cream by leaving the mush outside in freezing temperatures to crystallize.

Families worked hard to lay by a large store of seeds for winter. In a good year, a family of four could gather perhaps 1,200 pounds of pine nuts in a few weeks of harvesting. Loath to carry such heavy loads, people generally stored their take close to the piñon groves. Some camped nearby for the winter; others settled some distance away and had to make dozens of arduous treks from camp to cache and back again to meet their needs through the cold months ahead.

Autumn was also a prime season for hunting. In the Basin, this was the best time for communal rabbit drives; the animals were plump from the summer's bounty, and their fur was thick and glossy against the coming winter, making the pelts ideal for the rabbit-skin blankets and robes that protected Basin dwellers from the cold. For rabbit drives, most tribes used nets measuring 100 feet or more in length and woven of twisted plant fibers—or in some cases, human hair. Several people stretched out the net and staked it upright like a long fence, while others waited with clubs along its length. Then the drivers approached from a distance, beating the brush with sticks to send jack rabbits bounding in panic toward the net. (Cottontails plunged down the nearest hole, instead, and so were hunted by other means.) As each animal hit the net and became entangled, a hunter quickly killed it before it could tear the cords. A good day's drive might net thousands of rabbits, enough for a big communal feast and a generous allotment for each family participating.

For some groups, the rabbit drive was a major gathering, much like the get-togethers at fishing-and-fowling spots or piñon groves. Northern

Paiutes staged big five-day drives, praying at the outset of each day. In some cases, they dispensed with nets and instead formed a circle composed of scores of hunters and slowly tightened it, clubbing to death the animals caught in the middle.

In this same season, many Plateau tribes were enjoying the best fishing of the year. Moving down the Columbia River in October 1805, Lewis and Clark found the shores dotted with drying racks, all laden with salmon. The fish choked the clear waters and were plainly visible down to a depth of 20 feet. So abundant were the salmon, said Clark, that the Indians "often use dried fish as fuel for the common occasions of cooking."

Few tribes had better fishing than the Nez Percé, who took from their many Plateau streams four kinds of salmon and as many types of trout,

Wearing the European-style clothing that many Washoes adopted when whites over-ran their territory in the mid-1800s, men of the tribe hold poles used to knock cones from the piñon trees, while the women move through the grove to collect the harvest. Traditionally, the pine nuts extracted from the cones were the primary source of sustenance for tribes of the Great Basin.

along with whitefish, sturgeon, squawfish, and lamprey. By one estimate, the Nez Percé annually consumed up to 400 pounds of fish per person. One early Catholic missionary on the Plateau, Father Nicolas Point, complained that the fishing was too easy for a neighboring tribe, the Coeur d'Alene, because it left them free to gamble, dance, and engage in other festivities that Indians considered spiritually significant but that Christians often dismissed as ungodly. The prevalence of such "vices," Father Point insisted, was "in large measure due to the ease with which the Coeur d'Alenes procure the necessities of life."

For the mounted peoples of the Basin and the Plateau, autumn was a good time to pursue buffalo, for the animals were at their meatiest after grazing through the summer. Utes headed out onto the central Plains, while Bannocks, Shoshones, and eastern Plateau Indians such as the Flatheads, Kootenais, and Nez Percés fanned out across the grasslands of Wyoming and Montana. The Kootenais, who were equipped with sinew-strengthened bows made of cedar or cherry wood, threw out in advance of their main party a wide ring of scouts, who signaled when they spotted bison. In early times, some herds on the Plains were so huge that Indians miles away could hear the animals moving, or feel the vibration through

Plying bark canoes much like those that were used for countless generations by their ancestors, fishermen take to the waters near a Kalispel village in 1910.

the earth. Faced with such abundance, hunters sometimes had to limit their take to avoid culling more animals than they could efficiently process. A Kootenai normally killed no more than two buffalo a day, since that was all his wife could skin, dismember, and dry in one day as she prepared meat, hide, horns, bones, and other usable parts for the journey home.

Buffalo hunting not only enriched the diet, it endowed tribes with new dwellings and modes of dress. Originally, the Basin dwellers lived either in conical huts made of poles and sheathed with grass or reeds, or in some kind of earth-covered structure. But once they became mounted bison hunters, Utes, Bannocks, and Northern and Eastern Shoshones all adopted buffalo-hide tipis, which had the advantage of being weathertight and portable. Mounted Plateau tribes generally used tipis in the warmer months but retreated in winter to their traditional lodges, some of them earth covered. In clothing, too, the mounted Basin tribes departed from the original pattern of their region—woven-fiber breechcloths for men and front-and-back aprons for women, covered in cold weather by rabbit-skin robes. Thanks to the horse, which gave them readier access to deer and elk as well as bison, the men took to buckskin shirts, leather leggings, and fur caps, while women donned buckskin dresses over leggings. Both sexes favored warm winter robes taken from buffalo or other big game. On the Plateau, where deer and elk were more plentiful than on the Basin, many tribes had long worn buckskin clothing. But with horses, they too adopted buffalo robes and other elements of Plains-style dress.

In addition to being the means by which good things were acquired, horses were also an end in themselves—esteemed tokens of success. Among mounted Shoshones, herds were amassed not only by chiefs but by prominent shamans, midwives, gamblers, and racers as well, who claimed their earnings in ponies. The Plateau's Kootenais rightfully considered themselves rich in horses, possessing on average about three to five per person. But the Nez Percés and neighboring Cayuses were even richer, boasting five to seven horses for each man, woman, and child. Because of the honor that was conferred by the animals, tribes in the region used them not only for trade but also for important gifts, such as that offered by a man to the father of his would-be bride. Horses were at the heart of camp life, as evidenced by bands that pitched their tents in a circle, with the finest mounts sheltered in their midst. And the foaling of mares in the early spring marked the promising dawn of a new year—a sure sign that the tribe would grow in prosperity as fresh shoots of grass poked through the melting snow and the colts found their legs.

In their life's journey from infancy through adulthood as in their movement through the seasons, the tribes of the western range adhered to traditions that were similar in many respects and distinct in others. All peoples of the region, for example, observed ritual precautions before, during, and after the birth of a child to protect the newborn and keep the powers associated with the mother's fertility from impairing the men and their ability to hunt. In many places, a pregnant woman and her helpers went off to a birthing hut outside the village. An elderly Paiute woman related to an interviewer in the early 1900s that after repairing to her *karnee,* or birthing hut, she did not see her husband or any male relative for 22 days. Nor did she see the village's medicine man: "He was the doctor for all sickness, but he knew nothing about babies coming into the world nor did he want to know about such things. Men were afraid of women's blood." Washoe women delivered at home, but they and their helpers were expected to ward off misfortune by performing no fewer than 50 distinct ritual acts. Washoes gave birth lying facedown, while a Flathead woman went into labor crouching with her hands on a post and her back to a female relative, who held her firmly around the waist during delivery.

Both Ute and Washoe women spent a month or more recovering from childbirth, during which time they lay on pallets atop "hot beds"—pits filled with heated sand by the Washoes, and hot ashes by the Utes. Among Utes, the father, too, recovered on a hot bed for four days. Flatheads, on the other hand, believed that two days was sufficient recovery time after birth; a woman who rested longer was thought to be malingering. Shoshones on the trail could get by with even less than that, as demonstrated by the pregnant woman who left an expedition and disappeared into the brush, saying that she would catch up before long. An hour later she rejoined her party, carrying her newborn infant and seemingly in fine health.

By and large, children of the region were warmly indulged as infants and toddlers, as were most Indian youngsters. Alexander Ross, the trader who spent time with the Okanagons of the central Plateau, observed that their children "are never weaned until they give up the breast of their own accord, or another child is born." Even the birth of another baby would not induce a Flathead mother to wean a child younger than three. Instead, she would nurse both of them, although doing so made her weary. Ute mothers breast-fed their offspring until they reached the age of four or five—by which time older relatives were acting as parents in almost every other way, as tribal custom dictated. Often, aunts, uncles, and other elders figured as prominently in the rearing of children as did mothers and fathers.

Umatillas gather before their winter home, a so-called longhouse framed of leaning poles and covered with mats woven of tule or cattails. Situated far from the Plains, Umatillas did not hunt buffalo and used such woven coverings rather than hides to sheathe their sizable winter dwellings and their smaller, portable summer lodges.

Despite the indulgence shown them, youngsters were expected to help with chores from an early age. Kootenai children began performing simple tasks like picking berries at the age of two or three. By six, Kootenai girls were helping their mothers dig up edible roots and carry water, while boys were joining in hunting and fishing expeditions with the men. The Nez Percé had a special ceremony to mark a six-year-old boy's first hunting kill. At 10, a typical Kootenai boy could make his own bow and use it to bag fawns and buffalo calves. Among mounted tribes, riding came naturally to the young. Infants were swaddled on cradleboards slung from their mothers' saddles. Toddlers were tied upright into saddles for long journeys. Children who were able to walk on their own learned to ride like adults.

Indeed, childhood did not last long in any respect. In most tribes, a girl was eligible for marriage as soon as she experienced her first menses—usually in an isolation hut removed from her village, perhaps with an older woman as her companion. Some groups celebrated the onset of puberty

Wishrams living along the trade corridor of the lower Columbia River displayed their wealth by endowing the brides in their families with lavish wedding headdresses such as that worn by the young woman above and the example at left. The long, white, tooth-shaped dentalium shells were traditional Indian ornaments; the dangling Chinese coins were the products of trade between coastal tribes and European merchant ships.

with dances. Among the Klickitats, the girl being honored joined in the dancing; among the Wishrams, she stood apart from the dancers and sang.

Marriage followed soon for most adolescent girls. Among the Nez Percés, when a young man took a liking to a girl, one of his older female relatives would meet with the girl's family. If the match seemed promising, the go-between would move in with the family to observe the prospective bride firsthand. If she met expectations, the union was formalized by two gift exchanges between the families, separated by about six months. Among the Washoes, an exchange of small gifts between families was enough to conclude the arrangement; sometimes, an elder marked the occasion by draping a blanket over the shoulders of the couple while speaking to them of their adult responsibilities. Among some Paiutes, the bride's father would inform his daughter of her duties while she handed her groom a basket of food, which the young man would take with his left hand while clasping her wrist with his right.

Relations between the sexes were not always simple or straightforward. Among the mounted tribes, where suitors often declared their intentions with a generous gift of horses, men who were more mature and accomplished held an advantage over younger, less-experienced males in competing for desirable young women. In their frustration, some young men resorted to philandering or abduction. Among the Utes, restless young males formed a society known as the Dogs, whose members wore wolf-skin necklaces, lived apart from the main band, studied the way of the warrior—and claimed the right to carry off and make free with any woman who laughed at them when they visited camp. Young Shoshone men who had no horses to offer sometimes stole unmarried women, or other men's wives, and made off with them to join other bands.

Although most tribes of the western range allowed a man to have more than one wife, and some allowed a woman to have more than one husband, plural marriages remained the exception rather than the rule. Among Utes, for instance, nine men in 10 limited themselves to one wife at a time. Some tribal bands looked kindly on polygamy only in the case of a man marrying sisters of another family. Among many groups, however, divorce was common, requiring as it did no ceremony other than separation. Most Utes married and divorced several times before they grew old.

By and large, people across the region defined themselves in terms of their family relationships—as sons and daughters, mothers and fathers, aunts and uncles. Outside the family context, there was often little in the way of social hierarchy to distinguish one person from another. That egalitarian streak was particularly strong among people who traveled on foot and spent most of their time in the company of close kin. To be sure, certain individuals within such tight-knit family groups were recognized as having special gifts—for healing, perhaps, or for communicating with the spirits of animals—and they often served as advisers or ritual leaders when bands came together in the winter or at seasonal foraging stops. But such groups had little need for chiefs or councils to direct their daily affairs.

In this respect, the Washoes were typical of horseless peoples. When they convened in large groups for occasions such as a pine nut harvest or an antelope drive, they readily deferred to the wisdom of elders and shamans. Yet their actions were governed not by civil authorities but by custom. If someone invaded what by custom was a Washoe family's ancestral pine nut grove, the family was entitled by custom to eject him and destroy his tools. Other Washoes would endorse their actions. In times of unrest, Washoes and other horseless peoples sometimes chose war leaders. But unlike mounted tribes that ventured onto the Plains, they seldom vied with distant enemies for resources and fought only sporadically over issues such as the abduction of a woman or the suspicion that one group's shaman had caused a death in another group.

Tribes that acquired horses tended to organize themselves into larger groups that required stronger leadership. Chiefs were needed to coordinate the sizable parties that stalked buffalo—and to deal with enemies encountered along the way. Typically the chief was appointed by a council made up of family heads, leading warriors, and other respected individuals. Among groups such as the Eastern Shoshones, whose fortunes rested heavily on such expeditions, a chief's authority might well endure from season to season and year to year. But any chief who lost the respect of his followers would soon be replaced. As Lewis and Clark observed of the sort of leader they encountered among buffalo-hunting peoples on the western range, "His shadowy authority, which cannot survive the confidence which supports it, often decays with the personal vigor of the chief, or is transferred to some more fortunate or favorite hero." The Flatheads were something of an exception in that their tribal chief, chosen by a council of "little chiefs," exercised influence that was far reaching and long lasting (for a time, the position may have been hereditary). When the Flathead chief declared, "I am going to the Musselshell River to hunt bison," listeners knew it was time for everyone to start packing.

Many communities on the Plateau were large and diverse enough to profit by the presence of a village leader, or headman. Among the Nez Percés,

UPDATING AN ANCIENT CRAFT

On the Plateau as elsewhere across the continent, Indian artisans responded to the arrival of Europeans and their trade goods by incorporating new materials and themes into their traditional handiwork. For ages, women on the Plateau had been fashioning twined flat bags, used to hold bitterroot, camas bulbs, and other roots they unearthed. The bags were made of strands of Indian hemp and grass, intertwined in geometric patterns. By 1860, however, root collecting was declining in the region, along with other traditional subsistence activities, as Indians moved to reservations. Many Plateau women began to use the flat bag as a purse for their keepsakes, and it became smaller and more decorative. Some wove these bags as before but enhanced the patterns with bright commercial dyes. Others made purses of canvas and applied glass beads to form colorful designs, many of them featuring floral or animal motifs. In recent times, Plateau artisans honored the past by returning to geometric patterns.

Most women designed these bags for their own use or as gifts and refused to part with them otherwise. As one Yakima woman put it simply, "They are too precious."

Deft of hand, a Cayuse woman weaves a flat bag by intertwining fiber strands. The task usually took a week to complete. Traditional twined bags such as the one below, made by a woman of the Spokane tribe, featured geometric patterns in natural colors.

Pictured in 1915, Yakima women proudly display their decorative purses, including both twined and beaded bags. The beaded bag at left, with a floral pattern, is one of the earliest such purses, crafted about 1860. Prized bags like this one and the later examples shown at right—created by Yakimas and other Plateau Indians—have long been exchanged at weddings and other ceremonies.

ELK WITH FLOWERS, C. 1870

BEAR AND MOUNTAIN GOAT, C. 1935

PATRIOTIC EAGLE, C. 1925

GEOMETRIC PATTERN, C. 1970

he was sometimes elected by the local council, which usually chose the oldest man in the community. In other Nez Percé villages, the post was hereditary, but the council members—basically, all the male family heads—could reject an heir they disapproved of and choose someone else. The headman's job was mainly to set an example of good behavior and settle disputes. He could always be overruled by the council. Some activities, such as warfare or buffalo hunting, required cooperation from a number of villages in a given area. In that case, the headman of the largest Nez Percé village usually became the band chief. For group action on an even larger scale, band chiefs and leading warriors of a region organized themselves into a council and elected an overall chief—or, in some cases, two chiefs, one for war and one for peaceful activities.

Antoine Moise—a chief of the Upper Kootenais, who became allied with the Flatheads during the reservation era—wears an imposing headdress, probably consisting of horsehair, in this 1898 portrait. Like other mounted tribes near the Plains, the Upper Kootenais and Flatheads evolved strong leadership traditions to cope with buffalo-hunting forays and the conflicts stemming from them.

Another form of distinction that men of the mounted tribes could aspire to was membership in an elite warrior society. Like their counterparts on the Plains, warriors in these societies prided themselves on behavior that might normally be considered reckless or contrary but was truly inspirational in battle. Among the Eastern Shoshones, warriors calling themselves Foolish Ones risked death by riding boldly up to well-armed enemies and striking them with purely ceremonial weapons such as a quirt or a buffalo-scrotum rattle. More glory was obtained by thus counting coup on a live enemy than by killing or capturing him (warriors shamed in this fashion were said to have been captured in spirit). The Kootenai had a similar society known as Crazy Dogs, whose members learned through visions to converse with dogs and fought with a tenacity worthy of their namesakes, never retreating and readily advancing in the face of fierce opposition behind their leader, who carried a 10-foot-long lance adorned with eagle feathers. Nez Percé warriors of a similar society each carried their own tall staffs, which they planted in the thick of the fray and stood by until they prevailed, succumbed, or were called away by their leader.

Made from the pelts of bear, ermine, and bighorn sheep and the split, carved horns of bison, this Flathead ceremonial dance bonnet conferred the spirit power of those esteemed animals on the leader who wore it.

Their discipline and dedication did much to make the Nez Percé one of the region's strongest and most influential tribes.

The same circumstances that offered warriors and chiefs the chance to distinguish themselves tended to increase disparities of wealth and status within tribes. Success in hunting and fighting brought a man not only praise but also plenty, in the form of horses, buffalo hides, and other prizes that set him visibly apart from men who were lazy or unfortunate. Mounted, buffalo-hunting bands were less inclined to share the take of their group subsistence activities than were bands that had few if any horses. Among the so-called Lower Kootenais—who lived at the western edge of the tribe's territory, possessed relatively few horses, and hunted deer rather than bison to supplement their salmon harvest—meat and fish were shared by all. By contrast, the horse-rich, buffalo-hunting Upper Kootenais who lived near the high passes bordering the Plains preferred to let each family keep what it caught.

Hunters who did well were still expected to observe rituals of hospitality, however. When a man among the hard-riding Flatheads killed an elk, he gave a feast for his neighbors. If he bagged several elk, he not only fed the village but gave away most of the remaining meat, putting only a little aside for his own kin. And the hunter who killed the first buffalo of the season shared it with everyone in his company. Such openhandedness earned the tribe the respect and gratitude of white visitors such as trader Ross Cox, who spent a winter with the Flatheads in the early 1800s and later avowed that they had "fewer failings than any tribe I ever met with."

However they distributed their bounty, the people of the western range knew that all blessings came to them from the spirits. Indeed, spirit powers dictated everything that befell humans, whether good or bad. Some Basin peoples acknowledged the two-sidedness of fate through legends concerning the fabled trickster Coyote and his trusty kinsman, Wolf (a creature known and admired by tribes throughout the western range before whites eliminated the animal from all but the northernmost forests). Southern Paiutes, for example, referred to Wolf as their "father" and credited him with creating the earth and the first people who inhabited it. As if envious of Wolf's accomplishment, the mischief-maker Coyote then saw to it that all humans would have to die.

Characteristically, Southern Paiutes and others across the region showed great respect for Coyote in their lore even as they portrayed him as the source of misfortune. Coyote brought death, but he also taught people to pray and enriched their brief lives by stealing fire for them and pilfering pine nuts from the first piñon grove to spread the seeds across the land. He disseminated people far and wide, as well. According to a legend of the Southern Paiutes, Wolf entrusted Coyote with a heavy sack, tightly bound at the top, and told him to carry it across the desert to Rabbit, who would know what to do with it. Partway through the journey, in desolate country, Coyote was overcome by curiosity. He opened the sack, and people streamed out in every direction. When Rabbit learned of their escape, he was furious: "Coyote, you fool, why have you done this? This is not where people should live!" Yet good things came of Coyote's misdeed, for with Rabbit's help, some of the people found pine nuts to eat and deer to hunt and prospered. To their descendants, that homeland was anything but forlorn. They considered it the very center of the earth.

Coyote did so much to make people what they are today that some tribes on the Basin and Plateau said that he had a hand in shaping the world and the human race. Others traced the miracle of creation not to an animal spirit but to a heavenly power identified with the sun or the sky. Eastern Shoshones referred to this great spirit as Tam Apö, or Our Father, and paid tribute to him in a sun dance much like that performed by tribes on the Plains. No less important in the world-view of many Basin and Plateau peoples was the maternal spirit associated with the earth. According to an Okanagon legend, the creator they called the Old One fashioned the earth in the form of a woman and made her the mother of all people: "The soil is her flesh, the rocks are her bones, the wind is her breath, trees and grass are her hair. She lives spread out, and we live on her."

Indians of the western range danced and prayed to these and other life-giving powers on important occasions throughout the year. Early each spring, Utes gathered to perform the Bear Dance whose purpose was to propitiate the creatures and bring hunters success. Many Plateau peoples hosted winter dances to renew ties with their guardian spirits—powers that often took the form of animals and first appeared to young seekers during vision quests. "To be successful," explained Mourning Dove, a noted Salishan chronicler who grew up in the late 1800s on Washington's

Presiding over the raising of a sun dance lodge by his fellow Kootenais in British Columbia in 1920, a medicine man in traditional garb stands in a nest at the apex of the roof poles with his arm aloft. In much the same way as they adopted material elements of Plains Indian culture, tribes of the eastern Plateau and Basin embraced the Sun Dance during the reservation era to affirm their longstanding devotion to a great and generous power in the heavens above.

Colville Reservation, "a person had to have power from a spirit. This spirit came close to its human partner every winter, and their bond had to be expressed at a public gathering where individuals sang the songs that had been given to them at the first contact with the spirit."

As part of the ceremony, hosts often celebrated the success that the spirits brought them by lavishing gifts on their guests. A man or a woman might don numerous robes, one atop the other, and dance amid the crowd, inviting guests to help themselves until the last layer had been taken. During this season of festivities, which continued for up to two months, people went from village to village, delighting in the generosity and devotion of their neighbors.

Although spiritual concerns often brought the community together, they could also cause conflict, particularly when a shaman was suspected of misusing his or her powers. Nez Percés on the Idaho reservation in the 1800s told of a malicious old shaman called Poor Coyote whose medicine was so strong he could kill with a curse. "He was powerful," said one tribal chronicler, "but he messed with the wrong man one time." That young man was a Flathead, who was passing through Nez Percé country with some horses he had purchased from Umatillas. One of his horses bumped

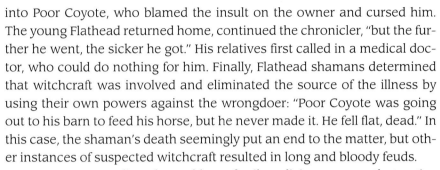

into Poor Coyote, who blamed the insult on the owner and cursed him. The young Flathead returned home, continued the chronicler, "but the further he went, the sicker he got." His relatives first called in a medical doctor, who could do nothing for him. Finally, Flathead shamans determined that witchcraft was involved and eliminated the source of the illness by using their own powers against the wrongdoer: "Poor Coyote was going out to his barn to feed his horse, but he never made it. He fell flat, dead." In this case, the shaman's death seemingly put an end to the matter, but other instances of suspected witchcraft resulted in long and bloody feuds.

However unsettling, the problem of evil medicine was one that native peoples had confronted since ancient times and knew how to deal with. But no tribe had an effective remedy for the terrible and mysterious diseases that swept across the western range from distant points of European contact well before the first whites entered the region in the early 1800s. One of the worst of these epidemics, an outbreak of smallpox, raged across the Plateau in the 1700s. Among the tribes ravaged were the Flatheads, who may have lost as much as half their population. The calamity occurred at a time when many groups were already facing sharp conflict with Plains tribes and other profound changes in their way of life occasioned by the adoption of horses.

Then, toward the close of the 18th century, an event occurred that struck troubled Indians as an omen. Part of the Plateau was blanketed by "dry snow," a fall of volcanic ash from an eruption somewhere in the Cascades. The phenomenon prompted some holy men to prophesy that the world would not last long in its present form. According to one prophecy, the creator, or Chief, promised to return soon to the earth and transform it. In the words of the Chief: "Coyote will precede me by some little time; and when you see him, you will know the time is at hand. When I return, all spirits of the dead will accompany me, and after that there will be no spirit land. All the people will live together. Then will the Earth-Woman revert to her natural shape, and live as a mother among her children. Then things will be made right, and there will be much happiness."

An influential prophet among the Spokane declared that this great gathering of souls would be heralded by another remarkable event—the arrival of white men, offering enlightenment. This prediction excited Indians who had heard stories of distant whites and their remarkable properties and looked forward to meeting with them. In due time, however, the tribes of the western range would come to regret that fateful encounter and long for the days when they had the earth to themselves. ◆

Young Colorado Utes celebrate during the Bear Dance, held in early spring. According to tradition, those who perform the dance—conducted to the rasping of a notched "growler" (above) on a metal tub—will be blessed with success in hunting and lovemaking.

Surrounded by her baskets, a Paiute woman (far left) sits outside of her winter home in southwest Nevada in 1924. At left, a Paiute couple build a winter home, tying woven tule mats onto willow poles.

THROUGH THE PAIUTE SEASONS

Endlessly resourceful, the Paiute peoples of the Great Basin exploited virtually everything of value in their stringent environment during the busy seasonal round. As winter set in, many bands came down from the hills to marshy spots, where they built or repaired their winter homes, made of willow poles covered with tightly woven mats of tule reeds. Women gathered the last of the year's bounty—including brown cattail heads, whose tiny seeds could be made into a gruel—and stored the seeds with roots and dried berries in underground caches. Through the winter, the women kept busy making willow baskets, while the men twisted strands of hemp into rope. Spring saw the return of ducks, geese, and other fowl to the marshlands, followed by the runs of spawning fish up the rivers. Paiutes gathered by the waters to fish and to hunt for birds, using newly made tule boats and decoys.

Come summer, harvesters combed the valleys, filling their baskets with mustard seed, desertthorn berries, Indian rice grass, and other wild growth. In the fall, people moved into the mountains, where whole families joined in the pine nut harvest. Women remained there for some time, processing the pine nuts, while men returned to the lowlands to hunt communally for rabbits or set snares for squirrels, rats, and other small prey that hunters in less stringent settings might well have ignored.

The age-old capacity of Paiutes to make the most of scarce resources helped them endure hard times when they were confined to reservations. Even though they could no longer range freely to hunt and harvest, they gleaned what they could from their surroundings. As shown here, Paiutes continued to draw support from traditional pursuits well into the 20th century.

Photographed in the 1890s, a Paiute woman in eastern California stretches willow stems between her teeth and fingers to prepare them for basket weaving—a common wintertime activity.

Renowned as basket makers, Paiutes made tightly woven vessels like this one impervious to water by coating them with red clay and hot pine pitch.

WINTER'S HANDIWORK

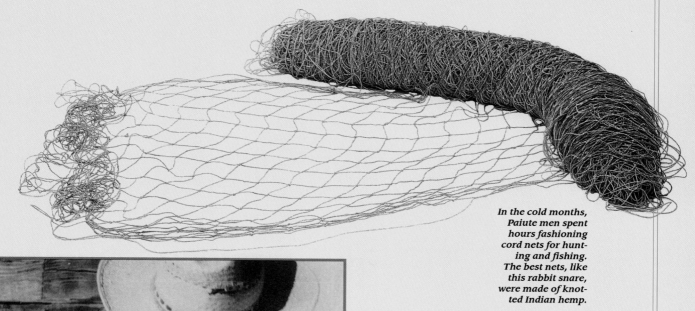

In the cold months, Paiute men spent hours fashioning cord nets for hunting and fishing. The best nets, like this rabbit snare, were made of knotted Indian hemp.

A 20th-century Paiute demonstrates the time-honored technique of rolling two strands of hemp together to make cordage, which was used to make nets as well as bags, mats, clothing, and other necessities.

In the spring, Paiutes carried bundles of tules from the marshes (left) and made them into rafts like the one shown below. A forager knelt in the boat (below, right) and poled it through the reeds, looking for duck eggs.

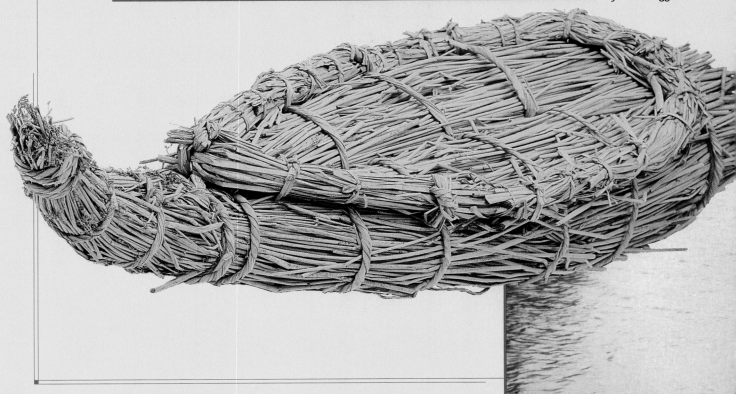

SPRINGTIME CRAFTS

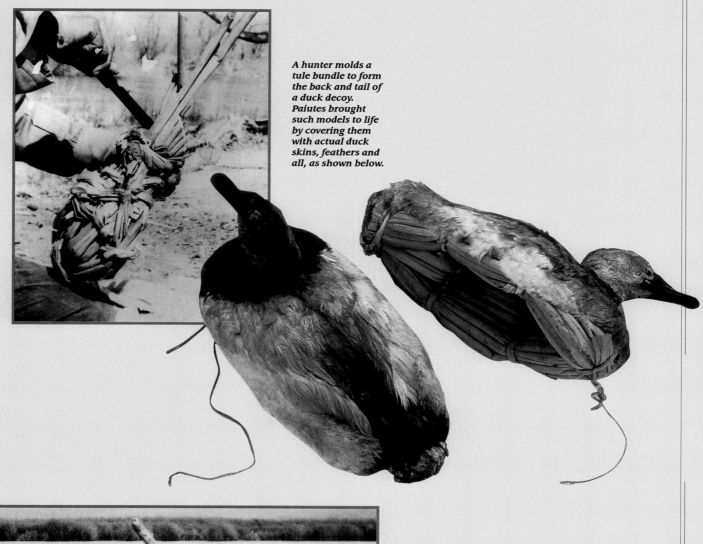

A hunter molds a tule bundle to form the back and tail of a duck decoy. Paiutes brought such models to life by covering them with actual duck skins, feathers and all, as shown below.

During the spring spawning run in 1950,
Paiutes use draglines with multipronged
hooks to rake in the plentiful suckers
known as cui-ui, native to Pyramid Lake
and a lure for pelicans (background).
In earlier times, cui-ui were speared with
twin-pronged harpoons (inset).

MONTHS OF PLENTY

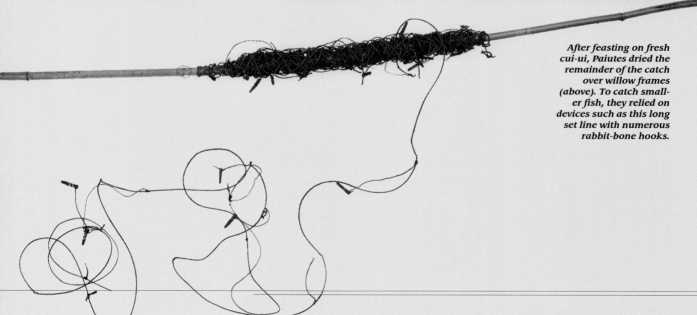

After feasting on fresh cui-ui, Paiutes dried the remainder of the catch over willow frames (above). To catch smaller fish, they relied on devices such as this long set line with numerous rabbit-bone hooks.

Heading off on a foraging expedition in 1872, Paiutes carry a variety of baskets to help with the task. Each woman has strapped around her shoulders a conical burden basket like the one at right, made to hold seeds and berries.

A TIME FOR GATHERING

Family members happily surround a heap of pine nuts gathered in north-western Nevada in the fall of 1912. The pine nut harvest was a time for hard work, relieved by games and celebration.

A harvester win-nows pine nuts to separate out the inedible hulls. The roasted and shelled nuts were then ground into flour between small hand-held stones and a flat rock (above).

Rabbit nets like this one were prized family possessions, kept in good repair for the autumn jack rabbit hunt. More than 100 feet long, the net was strung between bushes or sticks to snare the animals as they fled from a moving line of hunters.

After the hunt was over, the men skinned the rabbits carefully, keeping the pelts intact. Each pelt was then cut into a long strip and hung out to dry.

THE AUTUMN CATCH

Strips of fur from as many as 100 rabbits were required to weave a single blanket like the one at right—needed during the cold winter nights. Traditionally, Paiutes wore these blankets as cloaks during the day, as shown below by a group draped in rabbit skin for a ceremonial dance near Kanab, Utah, in 1872.

SPOTTED HORSES OF THE PLATEAU

In 1806, less than 100 years after the arrival of the horse in the Northwest, Meriwether Lewis, a skilled horseman in his own right, noted with admiration the vast herds of the Nez Percé. "Their horses appear to be of an excellent race," he wrote in the journal of his famous expedition with William Clark. "They are lofty, elegantly formed, active, and durable; in short many of them look like fine English coursers and would make a figure in any country. Some of those horses are pied with large spots of white irregularly scattered and intermixed with the black, brown, bay, or some other dark color."

The distinctively spotted horse, known today as the Appaloosa, evolved as a favored mount for the Nez Percé and other tribes of the Plateau. Carefully bred for performance by savvy Indian horsemen, the spotted steed remained unsurpassed for its speed, agility, and endurance. Indeed, the ancestral strain of the spotted horse has been held in esteem down through the ages, not only in the American West but throughout the world.

The spotted horse first came to the New World with the Spanish conquistadors, and followed the route of Spanish conquest and expansion northward through Mexico and into the American Southwest. The horses made their appearance on the western range late in the 17th century. On the Plateau, the gentle, grassy hills and sheltered valleys provided ideal, year-round pasturage for the thriving herds of the Indian horsemen for more than 150 years. But the encroachment of white settlers and the transition to farmland signaled the end for the great herds. During the course of the reservation period, thousands of the Indian horses were confiscated, slaughtered, or sold to ranchers far away. In a very few isolated areas, however, traditional Indian horsemen continued to breed the sturdy, spotted steeds. Today the horse, known officially as the Appaloosa since 1938, is enjoying a renaissance on the Plateau. Indian horse clubs, ranches, and breeders are using the unique horse to teach reservation children the equestrian skills so dashingly displayed by their forefathers.

Carla HighEagle rides a spotted Appaloosa on the Nez Percé Reservation in Lapwai, Idaho. HighEagle is active in the Nez Percé Appaloosa Horse Club, which sponsors the First Horse Program, providing children with instruction and Appaloosas to ride.

OLD WORLD GLORY

The T'ang dynasty sculpture of a spotted horse from the seventh century AD resembles statuettes buried with the Chinese nobility as early as the third century AD.

The first spotted horses may have come from central Asia because they made an indelible impression on the Mongols, Chinese, and Persians. By the end of the Middle Ages, horses with spots on their flanks or haunches had been depicted in the art, textiles, and literature of virtually every major culture from China to western Europe as the chosen mount of many emperors and nobility. In Spain, where horses were particularly valued by mounted soldiers, and later by cattle ranchers, horse breeders developed strong and speedy strains that came to be prized throughout Europe and later in the New World. The Spanish Andalusian horse, a breed frequently marked by a mottled coat pattern, arrived in the Americas with the Spanish colonists and was considered to be the seedstock for the Indian Appaloosa.

During the Middle Ages in Europe, a Spanish miniaturist illustrated a copy of Saint Bactus's "Commentary" on the Apocalypse of Saint John with four riders mounted on spotted horses.

This 18th-century Spanish illustration shows the technique used for winching a horse aboard a ship for passage to the New World. Only half of the horses that were shipped to America from Spain survived the voyage.

A MOUNT FOR THE AMERICAS

This pictograph on a canyon wall in Arizona shows a column of Spanish soldiers and priests; two in the center ride spotted horses.

Armed and mounted conquistadors made a terrifying impression on the Native Americans who first saw them, and the Spaniards tried to maintain this superiority by making it illegal for Indians to own or even ride horses. But inevitably those strictures failed to stand; the Pueblo Indians, many serving the Spanish overlords in menial positions such as stable hands, soon learned the art of horsemanship, and within a few years, they were acquiring horses through barter and theft and trading them with their neighbors to the north. By the 1690s, the Shoshones were exchanging horses at their annual rendezvous in the Great Basin and serving as middlemen supplying Plateau tribes. By 1750 the majority of tribes on the Plateau and on the Plains to the east had acquired the animal.

This dynamic elk-skin painting, attributed to a Shoshone artisan, features many spotted horses. The Shoshones' proximity to the supply of Spanish horses vastly bolstered their influence as traders.

The map traces the dispersal of the horse, from its arrival with the Spanish colonists in northern Mexico, to the southwest United States and thence up the Rio Grande into the Plateau region and the Great Plains.

1730 BLOOD
WALLAWALLA
NEZ PERCE
CAYUSE
1730
1710
FLATHEAD
YAKIMA
1720
BLACKFEET
1730
CROW
1778
1690-1700
SHOSHONE
1660-1690
UTE
1659
NAVAJO
1600
KIOWA
MEXICO

THE NORTHWARD SPREAD OF
HORSES IN WESTERN AMERICA

Migration of the
Spanish horses

Scale of Miles
0   100   200

THE LOST BREED

An early-20th-century Yakima artist decorated this beadwork bag with an Appaloosa and a smaller pinto, two breeds closely associated with Indians of the American West.

Beginning in the early 18th century, the Nez Percé along the Palouse River practiced selective breeding with their horses, allowing only the finest of them to mate and trading the inferior stock. Early explorer Meriwether Lewis found their gelding techniques to be superior to those used on contemporary eastern plantations.

Following the defeat of the Nez Percé in 1877, the U.S. Army confiscated the greater part of the tribe's herds, including nearly all their finest Appaloosas, and sold them to buyers in the East and Midwest. For more than half a century, the Appaloosa was a "lost breed" for the Nez Percé and other Plateau tribes.

In the early 20th century, the Nez Percé still had a few treasured Appaloosas among their stock. The photographs of two Nez Percé men seated before an Appaloosa (right) and a parade of Nez Percé women, two of whom ride spotted horses (below), attest that "a Palouse" (hence the name Appaloosa) was still a desirable mount.

Justin Rabago gets instruction from his father on bridling an Appaloosa. He and other youngsters in the Nez Percé community will grow up as horsemen in the manner of their forefathers.

Mario Rabago, a member of the Chief Joseph Foundation, exercises an Appaloosa at the foundation's Lapwai headquarters.

REBUILDING TRADITION

Carla HighEagle leads her Appaloosa in full regalia with Teresa and Tyler HighEagle aboard.

In 1991 a New Mexico rancher and Appaloosa lover gave the Lapwai reservation 13 fine Appaloosa mares in an effort to help restore the depleted herds of the Nez Percé and thereby reestablish the tribe as premier horse breeders.

A generation of youngsters had grown up largely unaware of horses and their historical significance to their tribe. Now, thanks to the Chief Joseph Foundation and the Nez Percé Appaloosa Horse Club, the community is acquainting a new generation with its heritage of horsemanship. At the same time, the Nez Percé are reclaiming their past glory and creating a new source of income for the community by giving the Appaloosa the prominence it formerly had in the life of the tribe.

2

ALIENS IN THEIR OWN DOMAIN

What seems to be a fort occupied by top-hatted white men is surrounded by the tipis of an Indian village in a pictograph by an Indian artist of the Plateau. The drawing was collected by Nicolas Point, a Jesuit priest who helped establish the first Roman Catholic missions to the Indians of the Columbia Plateau during the 1840s.

Year after year, Northern Shoshones made their way through passes in the Rockies to hunt on the grasslands to their east, in what is now Montana. There beyond the watershed known today as the Continental Divide, bison grazed in numbers unrivaled in the rugged Shoshone homeland. Yet the hazards of the journey were as great as the rewards. Hunting parties that crossed the mountains to pursue the herds risked being stalked themselves by raiders from hostile Plains tribes. Among those watchful opponents were Hidatsas, who rode all the way from their villages along the Missouri River in present-day North Dakota to ambush Shoshones, making off with captives and horses. While the isolated Shoshones were still relying on the bow and arrow, Hidatsas were carrying firearms purchased from white traders who began venturing up the Missouri in the 1700s. Few Shoshones targeted by those well-armed warriors ever saw their homeland again.

Such was the fate of a band of Northern Shoshone hunters who camped with their families about the year 1800 at Three Forks, where the headwaters of the Missouri River converge in southwestern Montana. The Shoshones spotted Hidatsas approaching their camp and fled, seeking refuge in the woods nearby. But the raiders pursued them and attacked, killing a number of people and taking some of the children captive. One girl abducted by the Hidatsas was fortunate enough to return several years later as part of a peaceful expedition that would have a profound impact on the Shoshones and their neighbors on the western range. Her captors called her Bird Woman, or Sacajawea.

A few years after she was captured, while still in her early teens, Sacajawea and another Shoshone named Otter Woman were acquired as wives by Toussaint Charbonneau, a French Canadian nearly three times Sacajawea's age. Charbonneau was a veteran fur trapper, trader, and interpreter who lived among the Hidatsas, from whom he either purchased Sacajawea or won her by gambling. Late in 1804, she was pregnant with her first child when a party of explorers sent by the United States government went into winter quarters near the villages of the Hidatsa and neighboring Mandan peoples. Formally named the Corps of Discovery, the party was headed by Meriwether Lewis and William Clark.

The Lewis and Clark expedition, as it would be known, had been commissioned by President Thomas Jefferson to explore the largely uncharted region extending westward from the upper Missouri River to the Columbia River and on to the Pacific Ocean. Jefferson hoped the venture would promote American trade with the tribes encountered along the way while strengthening U.S. claims to a region contested by other nations. Although France had recently ceded its territory in the West to the United States through the Louisiana Purchase, Great Britain was vying for control of much of the country that Lewis and Clark would traverse, while Spain and Russia had interests there as well.

Before setting out again in the spring of 1805, Lewis and Clark hired Charbonneau as an interpreter—and received a bonus in the person of the 16-year-old Sacajawea. She was now the mother of a baby boy, Jean-Baptiste, born on February 11. To ease her labor, she had tried an old Indian remedy, a mixture made by grinding the rattles from snakes into a powder that she dissolved in water. Within 10 minutes of taking the mixture, Sacajawea had given birth. Lewis and Clark realized that even with the baby, Sacajawea would prove valuable. The Shoshones had horses that the explorers would need to haul their gear over the mountains from the Missouri to the Columbia. Sacajawea could interpret and perhaps intercede with her people. Thus, when the party of 33 broke camp on April 7, 1805, and proceeded up the Missouri in a fleet of six canoes equipped with sails, there were two Indians among them—Sacajawea and Jean-Baptiste, riding in a cradleboard on her back.

From the start, she demonstrated her mettle, enduring hardship without complaint and proving ever resourceful. Two days into the journey, she went out in the evening with a digging stick of the kind Shoshone women had long used to unearth edible roots. Prying into gopher holes along the riverbank, she extracted tubers the gophers hoarded that resembled Jerusalem artichoke and brought the nutritious vegetables back for dinner. A month or so later, while the canoes were traveling under sail in eastern Montana, her husband lost control of his vessel's rudder in a squall and the boat nearly capsized. Charbonneau panicked and had to be threatened with a gun before he grasped the rudder and steadied the vessel. Meanwhile, Sacajawea sat calmly in the stern, up to her waist in water, and retrieved much of the gear that had spilled overboard. The equipment she salvaged included instruments, books, medicine, and trade goods—in short, "almost every article indispensable to our enterprise," according to Lewis. A few days later, the explorers honored her "fortitude and resolution" by naming a tributary of the Missouri the Bird Woman River.

Later Sacajawea raised everyone's spirits when she recognized landmarks near the headwaters of the Missouri. On July 28, the party camped at Three Forks, where she told of her capture as a child. "I cannot discover that she shows any emotion of sorrow in recollecting this event, or of joy in being restored to her native country," wrote Lewis. "If she has enough to eat and a few trinkets to wear, I believe she would be perfectly content anywhere." In truth, she remained deeply attached to her country and kin, as would soon become clear.

In early August, as the expedition probed for a pass through the Rockies, Sacajawea recognized from afar Beaverhead Rock, a landmark for Northern Shoshones who crossed over from the west to hunt. It was none

In an 1870 photograph, Shoshones meet in Wyoming's Wind River valley, southeast of where the Lewis and Clark expedition encountered a Shoshone band 65 years before. For their trek across the Rockies, the explorers received invaluable assistance from a young Shoshone woman named Sacajawea.

too soon. The explorers had not met with any Indians since departing winter camp four months earlier, and they were in desperate need of horses. The headwaters of the Missouri were growing ever shallower, and soon the boats would have to be abandoned. Lewis went ahead with a small party, while Sacajawea stayed behind with Clark and the rest. On August 12, members of the advance party crossed the Continental Divide at Lemhi Pass and descended into present-day Idaho, where they encountered Shoshones camped near the Lemhi River. The men there embraced the white strangers heartily and gladly accepted Lewis's offering of a peace pipe, after first removing their moccasins to signify that they would go barefoot thereafter if they failed to speak truly. It was readily apparent why the Shoshones risked forays into Montana to hunt bison: They were lean with hunger and could offer their guests little more than dried berries to eat. One villager, however, kindly offered Lewis a piece of fresh-roasted salmon—a sure sign that the explorers had reached waters flowing to the Pacific.

Communicating through signs, Lewis persuaded the chief of the camp, Cameahwait, and many of his people to return with the advance party to the east side of the divide, where they would rendezvous with Clark and company. When the two groups first made contact on August 16, Sacajawea literally danced with joy at seeing some Shoshones who were riding out ahead of Lewis's party. Then, on the following day, she was reunited with other familiar figures, including a young woman who had been captured by Hidatsas at the same time as Sacajawea but had managed to escape. An even greater surprise awaited her that evening. When Clark met with Cameahwait and Lewis, she was called in to translate the chief's remarks into Hidatsa for Charbonneau, whose French would then be rendered into English by another translator. After entering the lodge and taking her place, Sacajawea looked up and recognized Cameahwait as her brother.

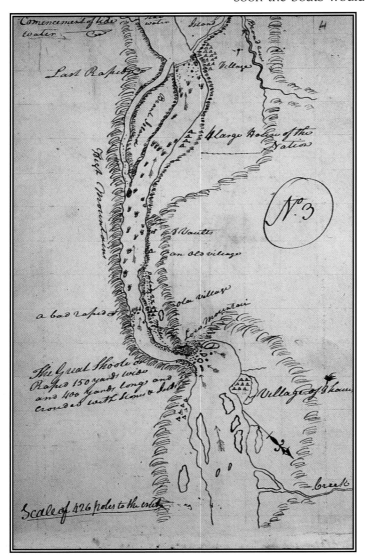

A map drawn by William Clark shows the Great Rapids of the Columbia River that the explorers navigated in canoes in 1806. Clark also indicated the presence of Indian villages.

Explorer Meriwether Lewis wears an ornate cape of otter skin decorated with ermine fur and abalone shells—"the most elegant piece of Indian dress I ever saw," he boasted—in a portrait painted after the expedition had returned to Saint Louis in 1807. During their trip, Lewis and Clark collected native artifacts, including the woven grass bag at right, a type made by the closely related Wasco and Wishram peoples of the Columbia River area.

She ran to her kinsman and embraced him, throwing her blanket over him in an exuberant gesture of affection and weeping profusely. After a while, she resumed her task as interpreter, an observer noted, "but her new situation seemed to overpower her, and she was frequently interrupted by her tears."

Sacajawea met with someone else of significance at the gathering—her intended Shoshone husband. A man twice her age, he had claimed her when she was a child by offering her father a handsome gift of horses; according to tribal custom, a girl thus betrothed would remain with her family until she reached puberty, when her father would send her off to her husband, often with a present equal in value to the gift received. As it happened, Sacajawea had been captured before coming of age. By the time she returned, her would-be Shoshone husband already had two wives; when he discovered that she had a child by Charbonneau, he relinquished his claim, and she chose to stay with the expedition.

Reassured by the presence of Sacajawea—and by Lewis and Clark's promises of trade that would bring the Shoshones the guns they longed for—Cameahwait agreed to sell the explorers horses and supply them with guides for the arduous trek westward. Sacajawea, with the growing Jean-Baptiste still on her back, received her own mount. En route to the Pacific, the expedition met with other Plateau tribes, including the Flatheads, the Shoshones' northern neighbors who sometimes joined them on hunting expeditions in Montana; the Nez Percés, whose women were busy digging up camas roots in the valleys of northwestern Idaho when Lewis and Clark passed through in September; and the Wallawallas of the upper Columbia River, whom the explorers met with in October as the

Indians were completing their fall salmon harvest and drying the fish on racks. To these and other tribes, Clark noted in his journal, Sacajawea served as a symbol of the expedition's good intentions: "A woman with a party of men is a token of peace."

To the explorers, Sacajawea exemplified the venturesome spirit of her people. After Lewis and Clark reached the Columbia estuary late in the year and began to send out parties to explore the coast, where whales spouted offshore, Sacajawea asked to be included. Speaking through Charbonneau, she told the explorers "that she had traveled a great way with us to see the great water, yet she had never been down to the coast, and now that this monstrous fish was also to be seen, it seemed hard that she should be permitted to see neither the ocean nor the whale." So reasonable a request "could not be denied," the officers concluded, and a few days later, traveling with Clark and others, Sacajawea saw for herself the vast expanse of the Pacific and admired the skeleton of a beached whale.

In the spring of 1806, Lewis and Clark returned east, following separate paths through the Rockies and across Montana. Sacajawea and Charbonneau remained with Clark until the two parties reunited on the Missouri and arrived back at the Mandan and Hidatsa villages in August.

Tara Snyder, a descendant of Lewis and Clark's guide and helper Sacajawea, brings flowers to a shrine located in Wyoming where, the Shoshone believe, the famous Indian woman was buried in 1884.

There, Clark paid a parting tribute to Sacajawea, declaring that she had served the expedition well and "borne with a patience truly admirable the fatigues of so long a route, encumbered with the charge of an infant, who is even now only 19 months old."

For her courage and grace during the epic venture, Sacajawea would long be remembered and celebrated. But a tragic irony underlay her contribution. With her help and that of her people, Lewis and Clark had succeeded in becoming the first white explorers to cross the Great Divide and reach the Pacific. For all the goodwill they displayed toward the Indians, their journey exposed the isolated tribes of the western range to future incursions that were seldom so benign. By amassing information about a region previously shrouded in mystery, Lewis and Clark opened the gates for exploitation. In their wake during the next half-century would come not only the traders the Shoshones and their neighbors hoped for but also trappers, prospectors, missionaries, soldiers, and, finally, farmers and ranchers. Ultimately the intruders and their fences, forts, and settlements would alter the character of the region and reduce native peoples who had generously assisted the newcomers to the status of aliens in their own land.

After the Lewis and Clark expedition, pressures on Indians were compounded by competition among outside interests. Protestant and Catholic missionaries contended for souls. British and American traders vied for the best pelts and for Indian help in obtaining them. Agents of the United States and its foreign rivals maneuvered for territorial advantages. When the rival powers came to terms, they drew up treaties that ignored the very existence of the tribal occupants, let alone their rights. After considerable dispute, the United States and Great Britain agreed in 1818 to joint occupancy of the larger Oregon country, which embraced much of the Plateau. Then in 1846, the two nations settled on the 49th parallel as the frontier in the Northwest, with the United States claiming the land to the south—an accord that drew an arbitrary line through the homeland of the Kootenai and other northern Plateau tribes. Native peoples in the Great Basin were subject to equally bewildering claims. The area was nominally under Spanish control until 1821, when newly independent Mexico took over. In 1848 Mexico ceded the Basin to the United States through the treaty ending the Mexican War.

Early on, the only competition that really mattered to Indians of the western range was that between rival fur companies. The first whites to

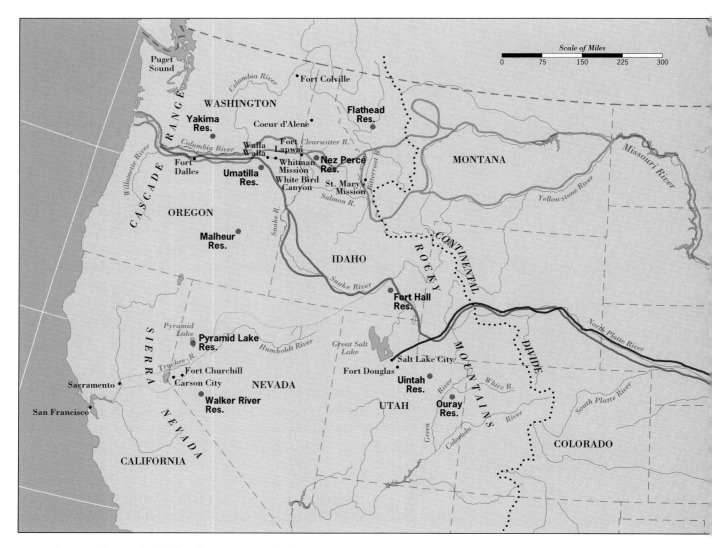

cross the Continental Divide after Lewis and Clark were traders and trappers seeking beaver skins. As it turned out, the rich, soft pelts, coveted for making felt hats, were hard to come by in the arid Basin, and the Plateau, with its many rivers and lakes, became the focus of activity. In 1807, less than a year after Lewis and Clark returned east, the Canadian explorer and trader David Thompson, representing the British-owned North West Company, crossed the Continental Divide into British Columbia and worked his way south. He established trading posts first among the Kootenais and later among the Kalispels and Flatheads, eventually opening trade with all the tribes of the Plateau and claiming the area for Great Britain.

Americans were not far behind. In 1810 Andrew Henry of Saint Louis built the first American trading station west of the Rockies—a cluster of log cabins in Shoshone and Bannock country in southeastern Idaho. The first winter there was so severe that Henry had to abandon the post. About the same time, John Jacob Astor, head of the American Fur Company, dis-

In the early 1800s, whites began to explore the western range and impinge on tribal homelands. Not long after Lewis and Clark pioneered a route to the Northwest Coast, other promising paths were being followed by fur trappers and traders, missionaries, prospectors, and homesteaders. Threatened by the rising tide of settlement, Indians who had first looked kindly on white visitors began to resist them. By the mid-1800s, army troops stationed at forts across the region and companies of white volunteers were clashing with tribes of the Basin and Plateau and pressing them onto reservations.

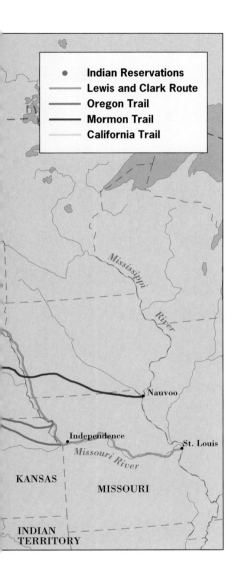

patched a two-pronged expedition to the Northwest by sea and by land. While the overland party followed the Lewis and Clark route westward, the seaborne expedition landed at the mouth of the Columbia River on the Pacific and made its way eastward. Soon, Astor's company had trading posts amid the Flatheads and Nez Percés, among others. After war broke out between the United States and Great Britain in 1812, Astor's interests in the region were acquired by the rival North West Company, which dominated trade on the Plateau until the early 1820s, when lively competition resumed there between the Canadians and the Americans.

The early fur traders on the Plateau tried to encourage Indians to trap beaver by offering them in exchange such alluring items as cloth, sturdy iron arrowheads, and firearms, which enabled tribes of the region to compete with their well-stocked rivals on the Plains. In 1810, not long after swapping with the British for their first muskets, Flatheads rode exuberantly into battle against their old foes, the Blackfeet, and won a rare victory against an enemy that for years had been better armed, thanks to their access to the Missouri River trade.

Much as they welcomed what the fur traders offered, however, many Plateau Indians who loved to hunt were loath to pursue beaver—an activity that seemed to them relatively tedious and unrewarding. Trapping beaver meant trekking for miles along streams seeking telltale signs of activity such as gnawed-off willow or aspen trunks. Even in good beaver country, the population might average only three animals per mile. In late winter and spring, trappers had to wade in icy water to rig their five-pound metal traps. They had to hide the traps below the surface, anchor them with poles driven into the bank, and bait them with willow sticks smeared with castor—an oily substance secreted by the beaver through its glands. All this effort yielded little in the way of nourishment. Although some Indians ate beaver meat, the main value of the animal lay in its pelt, and processing hides was women's work.

The Nez Percés, in particular, resisted trapping. They had horses to swap for guns and ammunition, and the men obtained ample food and clothing for their kin during their annual buffalo hunt on the Plains. "They spurned the idea of crawling about in search of furs," wrote the Canadian trader Alexander Ross. Such a life, they insisted, "was only fit for women and slaves." High-handed treatment from some traders also deterred Indians from trapping beaver and turned entire tribes against the intruders. In one incident about 1812, a Nez Percé was hanged for stealing a trader's silver drinking goblet. Word of the outrage swept across the Plateau, inciting tribes that already felt trespassed on by white traders or trappers. Indians began ambushing such interlopers or pilfering the caches where they stored their skins. In 1813 a group of Bannocks attacked and killed seven Canadian men who were trapping on the Boise River without tribal permission. In January 1814, another Bannock attack claimed the lives of several whites at their trading base on the Snake River. Only the Indian wife and children of Pierre Dorion, the party's French Canadian guide, escaped.

The North West Company further antagonized tribes by using its own men and equipment to transport furs from the trading posts to distant embarkation points, thus denying local Indians a share in the profits. Many tribes remained hostile until 1816, when the company agreed to let them serve as middlemen by conveying furs through their own territory. At the same time, however, the company introduced a new complication. Recognizing the difficulty of recruiting "refractory natives" to do the trapping, it brought in eastern Indians, mostly Iroquois, who had been trapping beaver and trading their pelts for centuries. By 1821 so many of these expert Iroquois trappers had migrated westward that they constituted nearly one-third of the company work force on the Plateau. Proud and independent—one white trader called them "quarrelsome and sometimes insubordinate"—they received a mixed reception from the Plateau tribes. Some groups accepted them into their families as marriage partners, but others clashed with them over women or over aggressive Iroquois trapping practices, such as taking beaver in all seasons regardless of age or sex.

Despite such difficulties, the fur trade flourished. The formerly gun-poor Flatheads and Kootenais soon boasted more than one musket for each man

Trading in pelts of the beaver, shown at left in a sketch done about 1700 by Charles de Granville, would radically alter the culture of western range Indians. The fur went to Europe, where it was made into hats such as the one being doffed by the dandy above.

and boy. Even the hitherto reluctant Nez Percés started bringing in beaver pelts to the expanding network of posts run by the North West Company and later by the Hudson's Bay Company, which absorbed the North West Company in 1821. Alexander Ross reported that his Hudson's Bay trading station in Montana, Flathead Post, did a land-office business late in 1824. He counted 128 lodges of Flatheads, Kalispels, Kootenais, and Nez Percés camped nearby—more than 800 men, women, and children in all, accompanied by several thousand horses.

Each tribe had its appointed day for trading, and much ceremony attended the event. When it was their turn, the Flatheads came up in a mounted body, chanting the song of peace. They halted a short distance from the post and discharged their rifles in salute. Ross returned the compliment with a salvo from his brass three-pounder. Once the smoke cleared, the principal chief advanced, welcomed the white men to Flathead territory, and apologized for the small harvest of beaver that year. Ross then invited the leading men into his hut to smoke the pipe, which was the signal for the entire cavalcade to enter the camp. Besides beaver pelts, the Flatheads offered buffalo meat and hides.

With wholesale prices for beaver hides soaring toward six dollars a pound, Americans began to reenter the trade. Leading the way were William Henry

Ashley of Saint Louis and partner Andrew Henry, who remained undeterred by the failure of his earlier venture in Idaho. Their Rocky Mountain Fur Company first tried to do business on the upper Missouri River, east of the Rockies. After failing to come to terms with the Blackfeet there, however, Ashley and Henry altered their approach, sending operatives over the Continental Divide to seek pelts at their source. These enterprising mountain men, as they were known, spent years in the rugged back country, supplementing the beaver that they trapped themselves with pelts obtained through deals with Indians.

Among the first to venture westward for the company was Jedediah Strong Smith, a clean-shaven, clean-living Methodist. In 1824 Smith led a party of six men over the Continental Divide through South Pass in Wyoming. That pass, long traveled by the Eastern Shoshones, would later become a vital link in the Oregon Trail, followed by tens of thousands of westward-bound emigrants. Continuing on into Idaho, Smith and his men stumbled on a group of Iroquois trappers stranded on the banks of the Snake River. A detachment from a larger Hudson's Bay Company expedition, the Iroquois had become embroiled that summer in a dispute with Northern Shoshone warriors over a woman or a horse—accounts differ. In the ensuing fighting, they had lost their traps, guns, and most of their beaver pelts. After listening to their woes, Smith relieved the Iroquois of their remaining 105 beaver skins in exchange for escorting the vulnerable Indians to their scheduled rendezvous with the main body of the expedition, led by Alexander Ross. Smith then accompanied Ross back to his Flathead Post in Montana, where the American shrewdly sized up the competition. By offering the Iroquois better pay, Smith's company managed to lure some of them away from their British employer.

In 1826 Smith led a pioneering venture across the Great Basin to California to explore the terrain and scout for beaver. He found that white traders had already made inroads on the Basin, but it was not furs they sought. When Smith's party approached villages of Western Shoshones and Southern Paiutes, the Indians were on their guard. Their previous experiences with whites, Smith learned, had been with Spaniards and Mexicans who came north for slaves. These outsiders seized Indian captives themselves—or more often, purchased them from mounted bands of Ute raiders—then carried the slaves south for labor in New Mexico settlements.

Although the Great Basin remained peripheral to the fur trade, some Indians from the area who had pelts, horses, or other goods the mountain men wanted joined tribes from the Plateau at a yearly rendezvous the

A large beaver dam crosses a placid pond that reflects the snowcapped peaks of western Wyoming's rugged Teton Range. The Tetons' green valleys were prime beaver-trapping grounds.

Americans staged. The inspiration for that get-together came from the Shoshones, who had long hosted an annual trade fair that lured members of diverse tribes. Beginning in 1825, mountain men gathered every summer along the Green River in southwestern Wyoming or in some other valley on the western flank of the Continental Divide. A wagon train of supplies arrived at the rendezvous point from Saint Louis and carried back the beaver pelts collected during the year. Soon Indians began to take part, and at its peak, the annual gathering attracted as many as 3,000—mainly Shoshones, Flatheads, Nez Percés, and Utes.

The rendezvous sometimes lasted an entire month. For part of the time, Indians exchanged furs or horses for tobacco, rum, firearms, powder, kettles, knives, and what the mountain men called "fofarraw"—alluring items such as ribbons, combs, and earrings. The rest of the gathering was given over to festivities. According to James Beckwourth, a celebrated mountain man born in Virginia to a white planter and a black slave, the rendezvous was enlivened by "dancing, shouting, trading, running, jumping, singing, racing, target shooting," and every other form of extravagance "that white men or Indians could invent." He noted that "the unpacking of the medicine water contributed not a little to the heightening of our festivities." Indians and mountain men took turns outdoing each other with gaudy equestrian tricks—and sometimes banded together to fend off raids by tribes hostile to one or another of the parties on hand.

The rendezvous encouraged trading partnerships between the Indians and the intruders, but the firmest alliances were fostered by intermarriage. The company policy of deploying mountain men in the wilderness meant that most would also become "squaw men"—the disparaging name whites gave to those who lived with Indian women. But mountain men valued their native companions. Some had several at the same time. The legendary Jim Bridger had three Indian wives in succession—a Flathead, a Ute, and a Shoshone. A trapper often purchased his bride from her father. In the process, the man pleased the woman's tribe and acquired a mate whose skills often included deftly preparing a beaver fur for market.

The qualities that endeared Indian women to the mountain men were the same ones they exhibited among their own people—strength, persistence, and a readiness to share with men the dangers of life on the trail. Trappers told of the courage of a Shoshone woman accompanying a party led by Canadian Peter Skene Ogden of the Hudson's Bay Company. Once, in the Snake River region, some rival Americans reportedly camped next to Ogden's trappers, got them drunk, and seized their beaver pelts, stampeding their horses in the process. The Shoshone woman was standing by her mount and had her bundled baby tied securely to the saddle when the horse bolted into the American camp. She chased after it, caught the bridle, and mounted up. Then she spotted one of her party's packhorses that had scampered off, laden with beaver skins. She grabbed its halter and, defying the Americans and their weapons, galloped away with baby in the saddle and packhorse in hand. Several men in the hostile camp cheered her along and told the others to lower their guns and let her go.

The competition between the Canadians and the Americans benefited Indians in the short term only. By the time silk hats replaced the beaver-felt variety in European fashion about 1840, the animal had been all but eliminated from the Plateau. The Hudson's Bay Company had set out to strip the region of beaver to keep out American trappers and protect British claims to the Oregon country. Undeterred, mountain men working for American companies took what the Canadians missed. Other game was depleted as well, as whites and Indians hunted for subsistence with firearms. A traveler among the Northern Shoshones would observe in 1843 that most were living on roots: "Game can scarcely be seen any more."

As the supply of beaver dwindled, American fur companies dispatched their parties ever farther afield—sometimes with dire consequences. In the summer of 1833, a group of 40 trappers led by Joseph Reddeford Walker left the Green River rendezvous, determined to keep going toward California until they found new beaver water. Near the Great Salt Lake, some friendly Bannocks gave them helpful guidance. Following the course of the Humboldt River through Nevada, the mountain men encountered Northern Paiutes, who sometimes hunted beaver themselves in the waters there. Walker's men jumped at the opportunity to wrest furs from the Paiutes for next to nothing; in one instance, they purchased a beaver robe worth more than $30 for two awls and a fishhook. But they reacted with fury when some Paiutes took beaver traps that members of the party were setting out. Much to Walker's dismay, unruly trappers murdered several Indians in retaliation.

A short time later, several hundred Paiutes armed with bows and arrows converged on the trappers' camp in the swampy Humboldt Sink. A delegation of their chiefs came forward and asked Walker and his men "whether their people might come in and smoke with us," wrote Zenas Leonard, a young trapper. Walker suspected that the Paiutes were intent on revenge, however, and declined. When a larger group of Paiutes approached later that same day, he told his men to brandish their guns,

RENDEZVOUS AT GREEN RIVER

Among the first whites the Basin and Plateau tribes met were the mountain men, those hunters, trappers, and traders who risked the dangers of the frontier to seek their fortunes in furs. Active only in the 1820s and 1830s, the mountain men relied on the Indians to teach them wilderness survival skills and to provide them with opportunities for trade and companionship, including the bartering of Indian women as their wives.

Lured west by the tales of these adventurers, a Scottish nobleman named William Drummond Stewart traveled to the area in 1837 to hunt and to attend the Green River rendezvous, an annual gathering of Indians and mountain men. Stewart brought along Alfred Jacob Miller, a Baltimore artist, to record his trip. In more than 600 works—four of which are shown here—Miller captured the ephemeral world of the mountain men, including their extraordinarily close-knit ties with the Indians.

As a gesture of friendship, a fur company agent hangs a beaded necklace around the neck of a warrior at the 1837 Green River rendezvous.

Indians look on as buckskin-clad mountain men prepare a convivial breakfast around a dawn campfire during the rendezvous. The trappers, after long and lonely winters hunting beaver, prized the Green River get-togethers as a chance to drink, fraternize, and court Indian girls.

TAKING WIVES AMONG THE INDIANS

Offered by her father, a shy Indian girl is accepted by a trapper as his bride in one of Miller's best-known paintings. About 40 percent of mountain men purchased Indian wives; this bride, the artist noted, cost the trapper $600 worth of trade goods.

Famous trapper and explorer Joseph Walker rides into the 1837 rendezvous with his Indian wife following behind on her pony.

which only seemed to amuse the Indians. The trappers then shot some ducks to demonstrate their firepower. Although the noise shocked the Paiutes, Leonard observed, they were so far from being intimidated that before withdrawing for the night, they "put up a beaver skin on a bank for us to shoot at for their gratification."

The following morning, Walker's party decamped without opposition, only to be hailed a short time later by Paiutes, who again asked the white men to stop and smoke with them. Walker feared an ambush and refused to be detained. When a party of 80 or so men advanced toward the trappers in a "saucy and bold" manner, as Leonard put it, Walker ordered a mounted charge. Few of the trappers had ever fought with Indians "and were anxious to try their skill," Leonard added. "We closed in on them and fired, leaving 39 dead on the field." Walker ordered his men to put the wounded Paiutes "out of their misery." Then the trappers resumed their westward journey, leaving behind them a legacy of bitterness.

Such bloodshed would become all too common in the ensuing decades as whites spread out across the Basin and Plateau in ever greater numbers. For now, however, the intruders were relatively few and imposed on the Indians largely through exchanges that left tribes in control of their territory but altered their values. Power and prestige came increasingly from outside the tribe in the form of guns and other prized trade goods. Since the Indians believed that all power was spiritual in origin, they welcomed holy men from the land of the traders. As they soon learned, however, those missionaries were not content to suit their beliefs to the needs of Indians but wanted to adapt Indians to Christianity by changing the way they lived.

Among the first to promote Christian ideas and practices on the Plateau were a band of 24 Iroquois brought in as trappers by the Hudson's Bay Company about 1816. These Iroquois had been raised as Roman Catholics by French Canadian priests at the Caughnawaga (Kahnawake) Mohawk settlement near Montreal. Led by an Iroquois known as Old Ignace, they intermarried among the Flatheads and instructed them in prayers and other observances, which gradually spread to other tribes.

Hudson's Bay officials saw profit in the conversion of Indians to Christianity. "I believe it would be highly beneficial as they would in time imbibe our manners and customs and imitate us in dress," wrote George Simpson, the company's governor. "Our supplies would thus become necessary to them." But rather than leave the task to the Catholic Iroquois, company officials chose to promote their own brand of the gospel. In 1825 they set out to recruit two young men from Plateau tribes for the Anglican mission school at Red River in central Canada. Tribal leaders, eager to please the company, responded with a number of candidates. The two selected were teenage sons of chiefs. Both were given the names of Hudson's Bay officials: Garry, a Spokane, and Pelly, a Kootenai. They proved to be such avid learners that in two years they knew enough about Anglicanism to meet stringent standards for baptism. Two years later, they were sent home to reacquaint themselves with their native tongues, which they had nearly forgotten, and recruit more Indian students for the Red River School.

Spokane Garry and Kootenai Pelly created a sensation back home. Wearing European clothing, speaking English as well as their mother tongues, and carrying leather-bound Bibles, they traveled across the Plateau teaching and preaching among the Nez Percés, Coeur d'Alenes, Flatheads, and others. Before returning to school in 1831 with five newly recruited chiefs' sons, they fanned the enthusiasm kindled by the Iroquois Catholics and inspired Indians to add to their traditional customs and beliefs such Christian practices as the sign of the cross, grace before meals, and observance of the Sabbath. Among those combining native and Christian customs were adherents of the so-called Prophet Dance, who prayed to a supreme God and sometimes confessed their sins but expressed their faith through their ancestral traditions of prophecy and ceremonial dancing. One prophecy originated among the Spokane Indians and promised that "soon there will come from the rising sun a different kind of man from any you have yet seen, who will bring with them a book and will teach you everything." Not long after those teachers arrived from the East, it was said, the world would end and true believers would attain eternal happiness.

Nowhere was the fascination with the outsiders'

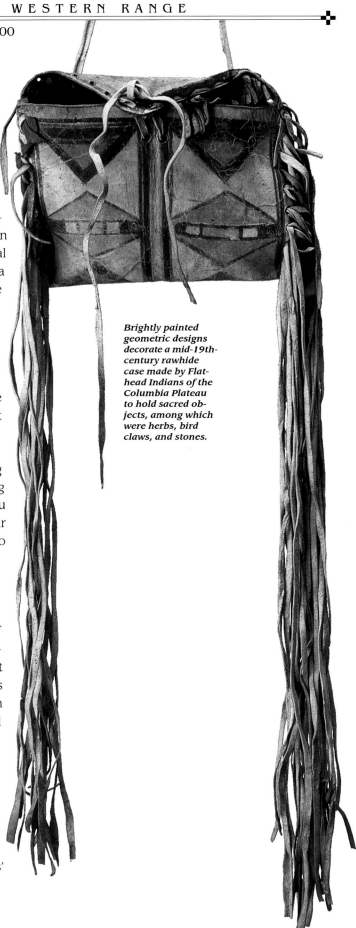

Brightly painted geometric designs decorate a mid-19th-century rawhide case made by Flathead Indians of the Columbia Plateau to hold sacred objects, among which were herbs, bird claws, and stones.

spirit power greater than among the Nez Percés and their neighbors, the Flatheads. They cherished the strength that came from traders in the form of guns and other goods and sought closer ties with the outsiders materially and spiritually. They were excited as well by the Spokane prophecy and eagerly awaited teachers from the East. Furthermore, the Iroquois leader Old Ignace had been urging the Flatheads to invite Catholic priests to come to their villages and show them "the way to heaven."

Seeking such guidance, a joint delegation of Flatheads and Nez Percés traveled to Saint Louis, where they met with two Catholic priests in 1831. The priests were gratified when the Indians made the sign of the cross and requested baptism, but it was some time before Catholic missionaries were dispatched to the Plateau. In the interim, Protestants learned of the delegation's visit and made the most of it. "Hear! Hear!" thundered the *Christian Advocate and Journal.* "Who will respond to the call from beyond the Rocky mountains?"

Among those to heed this summons was an adventurous Presbyterian, Marcus Whitman, who left his doctor's practice in New York State in 1835 and headed west as a missionary. That summer he reached the Green River rendezvous, where he performed open-air surgery on those in need. His most celebrated operation was extracting without anesthesia a three-inch-long iron arrowhead that had been lodged by a Blackfeet warrior in the back of Jim Bridger three years before. When Whitman marveled that the wound had not putrefied, the stoic Bridger reportedly quipped, "In the mountains, Doctor, meat don't spoil."

Some Indians present were impressed by Whitman's medicine and invited him to establish missions in their lands. A Nez Percé chief named Tackensuatis delivered an eloquent plea. According to a colleague of Whitman's, Tackensuatis "said he had heard from white men a little about God, which had only gone into his ears; he wished to know enough to have it go down into his heart, to influence his life, and to teach his people." Inspired by such appeals, Whitman returned from the East in 1836 with reinforcements. They included his bride, Narcissa, and the Reverend Henry Harmon Spalding and his new wife, Eliza. That summer the Whitman and Spalding brides became the first white women to attend the Green River rendezvous. They were in for a surprise when a band of 600 friendly Shoshone warriors chose to mark the occasion and display their horsemanship by staging a mock attack on the tents the missionaries occupied. Undaunted, the Presbyterians went on to establish mission posts about 100 miles apart—the Whitmans among the Cayuses on the Walla

Eager to obtain the spiritual power that they felt Christianity offered, Rabbit-Skin Leggings (above) and No Horns on His Head (right) participated in a Nez Percé-Flathead pilgrimage in 1831 to Saint Louis in search of Catholic priests to serve their people. These Plateau tribes sought to gain the protection against disease and death they believed resided in the white man's "Book of Heaven."

Walla River in southeastern Washington State, the Spaldings among the Nez Percés on Lapwai Creek in northwestern Idaho.

One obstacle they faced was the itinerant nature of the Indians, who traveled about in small bands in search of sustenance for much of the year. Convinced that people on the move could never be Christianized, Spalding and Whitman set out to establish permanent agricultural communities. Many Indians resisted. Breaking ground for planting was considered a sacrilege by some, who saw it as an affront to a nurturing earth that freely offered people sustenance in the form of berries, seeds, and roots. In any case, gathering such bounty had always been women's work, and men were reluctant to take part. Spalding nonetheless passed out hoes to the Nez Percés and persuaded men at his mission to cultivate 15 acres of potatoes, peas, and other vegetables.

Spalding encountered greater resistance when he imported a flock of sheep to teach his charges animal husbandry. The sheep fell prey to the dogs that roamed the Nez Percé camps and were cherished there as pets. Spalding tried to eliminate the dogs by putting a bounty on them for his

The sketch by a visitor shows the layout of the mission founded in 1836 by the pioneering Presbyterian missionary Marcus Whitman and his wife, Narcissa, among the Cayuse Indians near present-day Walla Walla, Washington.

followers to collect. Paying converts to kill village pets did not sit well with the traditionalists.

The missionaries encountered other problems of their own making. Stern revivalists, they branded as sinful not only instances of polygamy and sex outside of marriage but also such native customs as gambling, ceremonial dancing, and shamanism. They warned that sinners risked eternal damnation, but that concept was alien to the Indians and had little effect. Frustrated, the preachers sometimes resorted to punishment. Spalding, in particular, was a harsh disciplinarian who backed up his fiery sermons with force. He not only flogged offenders himself but induced reluctant tribal leaders to administer the whip as well. A colleague of Spalding's wrote that he justified this to the Indians by citing Christ's example "in making a scourge of small cords and driving the people from the temple." The Nez Percés, who seldom reacted violently to any offense within the tribe short of witchcraft, must have recoiled when Spalding punished people who were simply adhering to ancestral traditions. Yet it was a measure of their determination to remain in touch with the outsiders and their powers that these proud people tolerated such treatment.

An alternative to the Protestant missions soon appeared in the form of Catholicism. Spalding, a vehement foe of the Catholic Church, warned of such a possibility in 1836 when he wrote from the mission that "these unsuspecting sheep scattered over these hills will not remain long unnoticed by the devouring wolves." In 1838 the bishop of Quebec assigned two priests of the Oblate order, Francis Blanchet and Modeste Demers, to minister to the families of former Hudson's Bay employees who had settled with their Indian wives in the Willamette Valley, near the Oregon coast. Blanchet and Demers took this opportunity to visit no fewer than 50 tribes along the Pa-

Christianized Nez Percé Indians attend a funeral (left) about 1915 at a Presbyterian mission church in western Idaho founded by early missionary Henry Spalding. Above, one of Spalding's successors, Kate McBeth, gathers with four Nez Percé women at the mission school where she instructed them in such alien subjects as etiquette in an attempt to acculturate them.

cific Coast and in the interior. They spent two months preaching on the Plateau, impressing onlookers with their long gowns and their solemn ceremonies that vaguely resembled some of the Indians' own. Unlike the Presbyterians, who put Indians through lengthy instruction before baptizing them, the priests baptized first and instructed later, thereby gaining a considerable number of converts in a short time.

Indians of the region soon found themselves caught in a heated controversy between Catholic priests and Presbyterian missionaries. The first blow was struck by Father Blanchet, who drew up a chart that portrayed a Catholic view of mankind's spiritual progress through history. Scenes from the Bible and from the lives of the church fathers illustrated steps on a ladder leading to heaven. Martin Luther and other famous Protestants were shown as perpetrators of error. The chart had little relevance to Indians, but some of them whittled a simplified ladder on a long stick, with 33 notches for the years of Christ's life and 12 notches for the apostles.

Spalding, who claimed that he and Whitman were defamed along

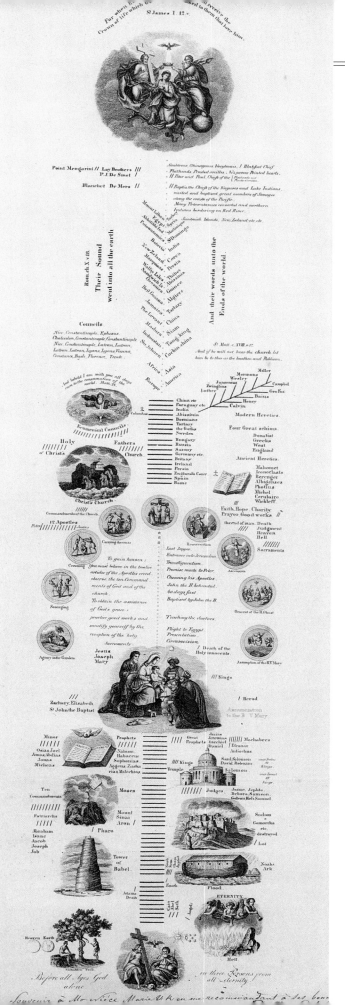

Designed to teach Indians the Catholic route to heaven, the ladder-like chart at left outlines the history and beliefs of the Roman Catholic faith. The ladder was first used by Western priests in 1838, then revised and signed by Jesuit missionary Father Pierre-Jean De Smet in 1843. On the upper right, the chart portrays Protestants languishing hopelessly partway to paradise on a dead-end branch.

with Martin Luther on a Catholic ladder he had seen, responded with a colorful chart of his own for Indians. Painted by his wife, Eliza, it depicted his own vision of mankind's ascent to salvation, replete with damning portraits of the pope and his followers. This bizarre battle of the ladders left many Indian viewers perplexed and even frightened. As prophesied, holy men had arrived from the East with books in hand, but they were spreading more confusion than enlightenment.

Some of the Plateau Indians got a clearer view of Catholicism in 1841, when the first permanent Catholic mission was established among the Flatheads in response to their repeated requests. The leader of this effort, Father Pierre-Jean De Smet, a Belgian-born Jesuit, first made contact with the Indians he was destined to serve at the same place Marcus Whitman had—the Green River rendezvous. There in 1840, Father De Smet was met by a deputation of 10 Flathead chiefs. Journeying with them across the Tetons to their summer buffalo-hunting camp in Montana, he baptized 600 Indians. The following year, he returned with two more priests and three lay brothers to found Saint Mary's mission among the Flatheads on the Bitterroot River, north of present-day Missoula.

Father De Smet's group—later augmented by additional mission workers, including a half-dozen nuns—went on to establish outposts among the Coeur d'Alenes, Kalispels, and Kootenais. But it was the Flatheads, already strongly influenced by the Catholic Iroquois, who evinced the most enthusiasm. "True children of God," in the words of Father De Smet, they fervently recited prayers and hymns and volunteered

In response to the Catholic ladder, Presbyterian missionaries Henry Spalding and his wife, Eliza, devised this chart depicting two paths leading upward from the Garden of Eden. Protestants ascending the straight and simple path to the right reach salvation, while the Catholics, with their ornate rituals, end up in hell (top left), where the pope can be seen toppling into the infernal flames.

to confess their sins every day if the priests so desired. Chief Bear Looking Up even offered to cede to Father De Smet his place as leader of the Flatheads. Later, when the priest told of hostility to the Catholic Church in Europe, the chief's son and successor, Victor, offered the pope sanctuary among the Flatheads.

Like the Presbyterians among the Nez Percés and Cayuses, however, Father De Smet considered the Flatheads' "inclination to a wandering life" an obstacle to his ministry. He noted that if they stayed three months in the same place, they grew "melancholy and morose." Perhaps hunger made them so, for only by shifting their base periodically could they get enough to live on. Every winter they had to embark on a long and grueling buffalo hunt. They invited Father De Smet to send a priest along with them, and in December 1841, he dispatched Father Nicolas Point, who held services outside his lodge every morning and evening during the hunt and asked God to grant the hunters success. Finally, on February 7, those prayers were seemingly answered, as the priest related in his journal: "At noon we reach the summit of a mountain, and what a change awaits us. The sun shines, the cold has lost its intensity; we have in view an immense plain, and in that plain good pasturages, which are clouded with buffaloes." In a single day there, the hunters claimed more than 150 bison. Father Point likened it to the catch the apostle Peter made when he cast his net at Christ's bidding and hauled in 153 fish: "The Flatheads confided in the Lord, and were equally successful in killing 153 buffaloes. What a fine draught of fishes! but what a glorious hunt of buffaloes!"

Such apparent godsends encouraged Indians to view Christianity as medicine for success in hunting or fighting. The religious fervor of hunters and warriors waxed and waned in proportion to how many buffalo were taken or how many enemy were slain. Although Father De Smet hoped to convert his charges from hunting and fighting to farming, he proudly cited their victories over rivals as illustrations of the power of prayer and "the special protection of heaven." At the same time, any concern the priests voiced for the souls of enemies angered the Flatheads. Once, when they had rival Blackfeet surrounded, Father Point insisted that the enemy be spared. The Flatheads obeyed "most reluctantly," a Catholic missionary wrote later, "and became highly incensed against the priest for meddling."

Indian resentment increased when practices encouraged by Catholics or Protestants failed to bring success. The Cayuses and Nez Percés, after being asked to make drastic changes in their way of life by the Presbyterians, grew uneasy when the hoped-for benefits failed to materialize. Farming yielded only grudging rewards, and the fur trade was on the wane. A further cause for worry emerged in the early 1840s as white settlers began to filter through Indian lands on the Oregon Trail. The emigrants were bound for the fertile Willamette Valley and for the Puget Sound area, and few settled on the Plateau. Yet the Presbyterians encouraged settlement there, hoping that white farmers would provide role models for the Indians and promote American claims to the region. Rumors circulated among Indians that the missionaries wanted to take away their lands. Returning from a trip east, Marcus Whitman came upon a wagon train of 1,000 settlers and helped guide them through the region, which only increased suspicions among the Cayuses that he had designs on their homeland.

Angry Cayuses and Nez Percés began to target the missions. In one incident in 1842, a band of Cayuses burned down the Whitman gristmill to protest the sale to emigrants of wheat and other food raised on Indian land. As the emigrant traffic increased, so did Indian anxiety. In 1847, a year after the United States acquired the Oregon country from Great Britain, more than 4,000 settlers trekked there. Cayuses complained that Whitman was more concerned for the emigrants than for the Indians he had come to serve. Indeed, during 1847, his mission often housed and fed groups of 50 or more whites who paused there to recuperate before pushing westward along the Columbia River.

Several of the travelers who stopped by in November of that year brought with them the measles virus. It was not the first European-borne epidemic to hit the region—deadly diseases contracted from Indians in

A watercolor by Father Nicolas Point in the 1840s shows the thriving Sacred Heart Mission in Idaho, complete with church, rectory, and numerous outbuildings. In 1859 Father De Smet (right), who served as a government peace commissioner between whites and Indians on the Plateau, accompanies an Indian delegation to a conference with U. S. officials.

A Flathead warrior known as Ambrose wrests a rifle from a mounted enemy in the drawing at left by the victorious Ambrose himself. After hearing Ambrose relate the tale, Jesuit Nicolas Point also depicted the warrior's feat (below) in a rare example of white and Indian artists recording the same incident.

touch with whites elsewhere had swept across the Plateau even before Lewis and Clark arrived. But this affliction appeared to many Cayuses to be Whitman's fault, for it spread from his mission school to their scattered villages. The Indians were especially vulnerable after a severe winter that cost them nearly half of their livestock and left them short of food. Those stricken were not helped by the traditional cure of visiting a sweat lodge before jumping into icy river waters. In less than a month, the epidemic claimed the lives of some 200 Cayuses, or nearly half the local population.

As a physician, Whitman tried to help Indian victims, but his efforts only heightened the fears of the Cayuses. By their reckoning, disease was transmitted not by microbes but by evil medicine. And the medicine man Whitman seemed to them a likely culprit. They felt sure of that after hearing the story of Joe Lewis, a mixed-blood employee at the mission. Lewis charged that Henry Spalding had visited the Whitmans and plotted with them to poison the surviving Indians and take their land. According to Lewis, Spalding urged Whitman: "Hurry, give medicines to the Indians, that they may soon die." Spalding may indeed have used words like that with the best of intentions, for he and Whitman were worried that more Indians would soon die and hurried off to give medicine to the nearby Umatillas, another tribe affected by the epidemic. But Lewis's report made such doctoring appear sinister in the extreme.

The Cayuses tried to test the truth of Lewis's story by asking Whitman for medicine for a sick child. After the boy took it and died, they invoked an old tribal rule: A shaman who used his powers to claim a life would have to pay with his own. To ensure that the harm done by Whitman and his kind would be expunged, they set out to kill not only the doctor but other whites at the mission as well. Entering Whitman's home on the pretext of seeking medicine, a chief named Tilokaikt—whose own child had reportedly died of measles recently—distracted the doctor while another Cayuse, Tomahas, crept up behind him and crushed his skull with repeated blows from a tomahawk; Narcissa Whitman was shot to death outside the house a short time later. Ten other whites staying at the mission were slain as well, and 47 were taken captive by Cayuses, who feared retribution and wanted hostages. The attackers also planned to kill Spalding, but a priest from a nearby Catholic mission warned him of the danger in time, and he and his wife escaped harm. (Spalding was initially grateful but later concluded that his Catholic rivals were somehow to blame for the attack.)

This was the start of the so-called Cayuse War. Soon all the missions in the Plateau closed down, although missionaries of various faiths would

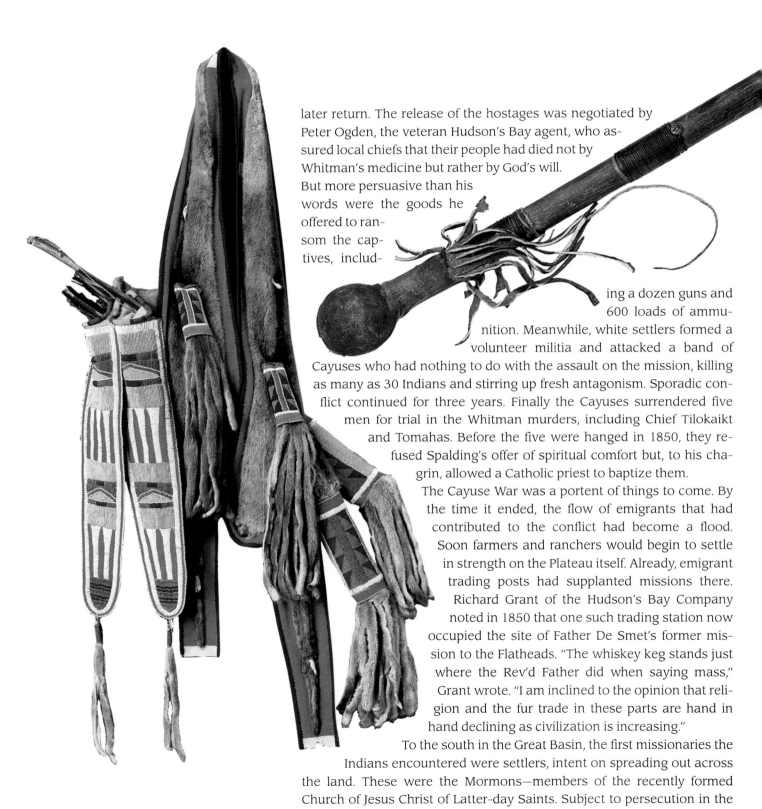

later return. The release of the hostages was negotiated by Peter Ogden, the veteran Hudson's Bay agent, who assured local chiefs that their people had died not by Whitman's medicine but rather by God's will. But more persuasive than his words were the goods he offered to ransom the captives, including a dozen guns and 600 loads of ammunition. Meanwhile, white settlers formed a volunteer militia and attacked a band of Cayuses who had nothing to do with the assault on the mission, killing as many as 30 Indians and stirring up fresh antagonism. Sporadic conflict continued for three years. Finally the Cayuses surrendered five men for trial in the Whitman murders, including Chief Tilokaikt and Tomahas. Before the five were hanged in 1850, they refused Spalding's offer of spiritual comfort but, to his chagrin, allowed a Catholic priest to baptize them.

The Cayuse War was a portent of things to come. By the time it ended, the flow of emigrants that had contributed to the conflict had become a flood. Soon farmers and ranchers would begin to settle in strength on the Plateau itself. Already, emigrant trading posts had supplanted missions there. Richard Grant of the Hudson's Bay Company noted in 1850 that one such trading station now occupied the site of Father De Smet's former mission to the Flatheads. "The whiskey keg stands just where the Rev'd Father did when saying mass," Grant wrote. "I am inclined to the opinion that religion and the fur trade in these parts are hand in hand declining as civilization is increasing."

To the south in the Great Basin, the first missionaries the Indians encountered were settlers, intent on spreading out across the land. These were the Mormons—members of the recently formed Church of Jesus Christ of Latter-day Saints. Subject to persecution in the

Weaponry of the Plateau Indians (left) included elaborate bow case and quiver combinations, made of otter fur ornamented with beading, and ferocious war clubs tipped with a leather bag containing a stone that could split an enemy's skull. At right, a drawing depicts the Cayuse warrior Tomahas, who led an attack on the Marcus Whitman mission.

East, they headed west in 1847 and founded a settlement on the Great Salt Lake—the future Salt Lake City—drawn there in part by the encouraging reports of explorer John Charles Frémont, whose government-sponsored expeditions earlier in the decade had mapped previously uncharted areas of the Great Basin. Frémont had described the arid sagebrush country where the Mormons settled as a "bucolic region," fertile and well watered. Once the Mormons were already on the trail, the old mountain man Jim Bridger warned them, "I would give a thousand dollars if I knew an ear of corn could be ripened in the Great Basin!"

American Indians had a special place in Mormon theology. According to the *Book of Mormon,* they were descended from a Jewish prophet named Lehi, who led migrants to the New World. Lehi's offspring divided into competing factions—the faithful Nephites, with whom the Mormons identified; and the unruly Lamanites, or Indians, who were said to have been cursed with dark skin because of their sins. The Nephites were commanded by the Lord to "go forth among the Lamanites, thy brethren, and establish my word." Lamanites who accepted God's word and converted to the faith would, it was prophesied, become "white and delightsome."

Beyond this spiritual interest in the Indians, the Mormons sought good relations with tribes in the Great Basin for practical reasons. They wanted to prosper in their new home without undue bloodshed. This position was enunciated by the pragmatic Brigham Young, who led the Mormons to Utah following the death of Joseph Smith, the founding prophet of the church. "We always consider it cheaper to feed and clothe the Indians," Young declared, "than to fight them."

A week after the Mormons arrived at Salt Lake, a band of Western Shoshones appeared there. They claimed the area as their own and complained that their old foes to the south, the Utes, were encroaching on it to trade with the newcomers. The Mormons helped arrange a peace council between the two tribes, but they refused a Shoshone offer to cede the place to them for guns and ammunition. Young's deputy, Heber Kimball, rejected the idea of paying Indians for land because it belonged to "our Father in Heaven and we expect to plow and plant it."

The Mormons intended to expand and to make this desolate region bloom through irrigation and hard work. Their hoped-for state of Deseret embraced much of the expanse transferred to the United States by Mexico in 1848, including Utah, Nevada, Arizona, and southern California. Although Mormons did in fact spread out across much of the Basin and parts of the Plateau, they had to settle politically for control of the Utah Territory, organized in 1850. Brigham Young was appointed territorial governor and thus became superintendent of Indian affairs there as well.

Mormons then dispatched missions to various tribes in Utah and surrounding areas to convert Indians and clear the way for settlement. In 1853 a corps of some 40 Mormon missionaries established Fort Supply on the Green River in Wyoming, among the Eastern Shoshones. That the Mormons came there to stay was evident in their supply train of 20 wagons, whose cargo included 75 pounds of seed wheat and 40 pounds of seed potatoes. Brigham Young instructed the corps to "preach civilization" to the Indians and to instruct them in farming and other skills, so as to "prevent trouble for our frontier settlements and emigrant companies." The Mormons later planted similar outposts among other Shoshones, as well as Bannocks, Flatheads, Nez Percés, Southern Paiutes, and Utes.

Brigham Young encouraged men who undertook these ventures to learn the tribal language and marry native women. Missionaries were allowed to take Indian wives whether or not they had white wives with them because Mormons then practiced polygamy, a custom sanctioned

Mormon elder Daniel McArthur baptizes a Paiute convert in a Utah pool, as some 200 other Indians await their turn. More than most white settlers, the Mormons adopted a benevolent stance toward the Indians.

by a revelation reported by Joseph Smith before his death. Not all chiefs were content to see their young women intermarry with the intruders, however. A Mormon delegation that sought permission to seek wives from the Eastern Shoshones was told that they had no women to spare. The tribe's principal chief, Washakie, invited the Mormons to court Shoshone women, if they wished, but only if Shoshone men were allowed that same privilege with white women. The Mormons declined his offer.

The greatest resistance to the Mormons came from the tribe that gave their home territory its name, the Utes. Young had been warned by Jim Bridger that they could be dangerous, and thus he attempted to placate the powerful Ute war chief, Wakara. Known to the Mormons as Walker, Wakara was invited to Salt Lake City, baptized in 1850, and even ordained as an elder of the church. But Wakara and his fellow Utes were soon provoked to the point of violence by two issues. One was the encroachment of a Mormon settlement—Fort Utah, later the city of Provo—on their hunting and fishing grounds and winter camping sites around trout-rich Utah Lake. Some Utes responded to the loss of subsistence by raiding Mormon herds. The other sticking point was Mormon opposition to the long-standing Ute practice of selling children they seized from the Southern Paiutes and other tribes to the white traders as slaves. By some estimates, as many as one-half of all Southern Paiute children were snatched away before they came of age. The Mormons denounced such slave taking on moral grounds and as an affront to tribes for which they felt responsible. In 1852 the territorial legislature outlawed the slave traffic.

By 1853 Utes and Mormons were at war. The Mormon militia mustered more than 700 men to oppose the Utes in this fitful conflict, which cost the lives of 19 Mormons and an untold number of Indians. In 1854 Wakara came to terms with Brigham Young, who offered the Utes guns and ammunition so they could kill their own game instead of raiding Mormon herds. A year after making peace, Wakara died and was buried on a mountaintop with lavish tribute of the sort members of the tribe reserved for great chiefs. Ten horses and as many blankets and buckskins were thrust into the burial pit. By one account, two of Wakara's wives died in order to accompany him on his spirit journey, and a boy and a girl captured from the Southern Paiutes perished as well after being imprisoned in a cairn atop the burial mound. Utes sang lamentations for Wakara for 20 days.

The Ute slave traffic soon ended, but a Mormon practice that had begun in response to it continued—adopting Indian children through purchase. At first Mormons felt compelled to buy young captives from Utes

Conciliatory toward the whites, Shoshone chief Washakie aided the U.S. Army in wars against tribal enemies such as the Sioux and Cheyenne. In return, he was granted a reservation for his people in their ancient hunting grounds in the Wind River valley.

who threatened to kill the children otherwise. But long after the Utes ceased to deal in slaves, Mormons were buying Indian children. Brigham Young encouraged the practice, advising his people to "buy up the Lamanite [Indian] children as fast as they could and educate them and teach them the gospel, so that many generations would not pass ere they should become a white and delightsome people." It was a special duty, in fact, of Mormon missionaries. But adoption rarely worked out as Young had envisioned it. Many of the adoptees either died of diseases contracted from whites or ran away. Those who remained often became servants to the family and were seldom accepted as equals.

Other Mormon efforts to convert Indians fell short as well. Missionaries rarely succeeded in persuading their charges to adopt farming. And while many Indians heeded Mormons and got "washed," or baptized, few embraced the faith to the exclusion of their traditional ceremonies. In 1858 Young was replaced as territorial governor and superintendent of Indian affairs by the federal government after he challenged its authority and defied U.S. troops. Thereafter, federal officials took charge of the material welfare of the Indians, and Mormon fervor to convert native people ebbed. Later, Mormons would reach out to Indians in new ways, inviting youngsters to spend part of each year with a Mormon family. Ultimately, the *Book of Mormon* would be revised to state that the goal of conversion was not to make native people "white" but "pure and delightsome." In the early decades of Mormon expansion, however, efforts to win over Indians were frustrated by the same obstacle that set tribal groups against intruders elsewhere—competition for the land and its scarce resources. Mormons concerned about wildfires even forced the Utes to stop their practice of burning away sagebrush to provide grassy open pastures for the game they stalked. Brush-covered valleys and plowed fields soon replaced the hunting grounds.

Mormons were not the only ones to vie with Indians for the fragile assets of the Great Basin. The well-trod Oregon Trail skirted the northern edge of the Basin, but in the late 1840s, traffic surged on a path to California that left the Oregon Trail at Fort Hall in southern Idaho and followed the Humboldt River through the heart of Nevada. In 1849, a year after gold was discovered in California, perhaps 21,000 people and 50,000 head of livestock trudged along this trail—with devastating effect on the Paiutes, Washoes, Western Shoshones, and other tribes in the region. Livestock devoured or trampled nourishing plants and grasses, and the emigrants themselves inadvertently introduced diseases, such as cholera, and deliberately harassed the Indians by taking shots at them or burning their villages.

By the late 1850s, the California gold fields were played out, but a newly discovered lode in western Nevada brought fresh swarms of fortune seekers. Behind them came merchants and ranchers who established permanent settlements to support the miners. The influx upset the delicate ecology of the western Great Basin, turning the California Trail into what one Shoshone referred to as "a river of destruction." The grasses, the game, the roots, the wood supply—much that had sustained native peoples for centuries was going or gone.

Selfless advocate for his people, the Washoe Indians, the man called Captain Jim served as a protective spokesman for the tribe in its dealings with the whites until his death in 1911.

The grievances of Indians all across the western range were summed up eloquently by Chief Washakie of the Eastern Shoshones. Speaking to Mormons who were ferrying emigrants for a fee across the Green River, Washakie protested: "This is my country, and my people's country. My father lived here, and drank water from this river, while our ponies grazed on these bottoms. Our mothers gathered the dry wood from this land. The buffalo and elk came here to drink water and eat grass; but now they have been killed or driven back out of our land. The grass is all eaten off by the white man's horses and cattle, and the dry wood has been burned; and sometimes, when our young men have been hunting, and got tired and hungry, they have come to the white man's camp, and have been ordered to get out, and they are slapped, or kicked, and called 'damned Injuns.' "

Washakie refused to retaliate against the intruders and managed to keep most of his 2,000 followers safely away from the emigrant trails. He did not trust those wayfarers or the whites who settled down in the area, but he felt sure that Indian survival depended on placating them. He was willing to endure affronts from white men, and even from some of his own young warriors, if that was the price for avoiding a ruinous conflict.

Farther west, the leaders of some Paiute bands and other groups pursued a similar strategy of accommodation. A few Indians even profited by the presence of so many intruders. One ingenious technique was devised by a Washoe leader called Captain Jim, whose homeland in Nevada's Carson Valley was swamped by silver miners. Captain Jim staged entertainments for the whites during the winter of 1857, using a novel variation on the tribe's traditional system of gift exchange. White guests were invited to watch the Indians perform dances and games and were even presented with a deerskin worth about a dollar. In return, guests were asked to contribute a sack full of flour worth about eight dollars. The flour provided a handsome dividend to the Washoes and helped them through the winter.

Sadly, few other tribes of the region derived much benefit from the outsiders through peaceful means. Many Indians were reduced to preying on the emigrants' livestock. For some of them, it was steal or starve. "Their voracity when they could procure a supply of food was almost incredible," commented one traveler among the Western Shoshones. "Five or six of them would sit around the carcass of a horse or mule and remain there until nothing but the bones were left." For people so desperate, defying the intruders was a risk worth taking. Before long, even Indians in remote spots who knew little of warfare would be banding together by the hundreds to defend what remained of their land and livelihood. ◀◆▶

A CLERIC'S LOVING JOURNAL

On August 30, 1841, a small party of Catholic missionaries under the leadership of Father Pierre-Jean De Smet brought their meager wagon train to a halt in the Bitterroot Valley, homeland of the Flathead Indians in what is now western Montana. The weary priests had traveled overland from Saint Louis at the request of the Indians, who wanted instruction in what they believed to be a most powerful medicine, the Catholic faith. De Smet's chief chronicler of the delegation was Father Nicolas Point, a Frenchman uniquely suited to the task. A self-taught artist and fervent missionary, Point was realizing his fondest ambition: to live among the Indians and do the work of God.

Since the exploration of Lewis and Clark at the beginning of the 19th century, few Europeans had traveled the area west of the Rocky Mountains. It was in this pristine environment that Father Point's talent flourished. His pencils and paints captured the daily life and spiritual culture of his beloved neophytes in a journal that is remarkable in its affectionate portrayals and meticulous detail. As word of his presence spread to neighboring tribes, Point was able to record encounters with Nez Percés, Kalispels, Coeur d'Alenes, and others. He often included himself in the scene, as shown in the winter meeting with a Spokane Indian at left.

The missions that were established by the priests—Saint Mary's among the Flatheads and Sacred Heart among the Coeur d'Alenes—enjoyed great early success. But in 1847, Point's health began to fail, and he was transferred to less strenuous duties in Canada. By 1850 the Flathead mission was abandoned. Subsequent displacement and disease brought on by waves of settlers and miners irrevocably changed Plateau cultures. But Point never forgot his followers. Toward the end of his career, he compiled his journal, featured here and on the pages that follow, from the hundreds of drawings, paintings, and recollections of the time he spent among the Flatheads and their neighbors. In many instances, they are the only visual record of lifeways that the missionaries felt spiritually obligated to change.

"Brief experience showed that Indians learned more quickly through their eyes than their ears, whereupon I made a great effort to speak to them through pictures."

Coups remarquables d'une chasse d'hyver. 1841 à 1842

Flathead hunters pursue a herd of buffalo during their winter hunt of 1841-1842 on this page from Father Nicolas Point's journal. The Latin inscription at the top of the picture reads, "Lead us on high"; the figure 153 commemorates the number of buffalo killed during that hunt.

A NOBLE PEOPLE

"I took up
my pencils and
attempted to
depict for them. . .
the most sterling
characteristics
of their
great men."

Victor, great chief of the Flatheads

A Nez Percé, admired by Point as "great in stature, courage, and authority"

Insula, or Red Feather, a war chief of the Flatheads

Kalispel warrior

Young Flathead man

Coeur d'Alene medicine man

A hunter reaches out to snatch an eagle as it swoops down onto the baited and covered pit that conceals him. This technique, sometimes described in the accounts of early explorers, is brought to life from Point's vibrant palette.

"The great buffalo hunt offers many scenes, one more extraordinary than the other."

"The best horse," according to Father Point, "is one which edges up closest to the buffalo without taking fright." In the painting above, a hunter overtakes a bison and prepares to fire a fatal arrow. The aftermath of the chase is shown at right. The Indians valued this animal above all others. "The flesh of the buffalo can take the place of all other foods," wrote Point. "As with bread, one never tires of it."

SCENES FROM THE HUNT

The winter scene above commemorates an especially fortuitous hunt during which a herd of deer, trapped in the snow, became easy prey for Coeur d'Alene hunters on snowshoes. At right, Indians gather waterfowl from an abundant lake. The plentiful birds could be captured by hand during the spring when molting impeded their ability to fly.

Children spin tops and play on the ice near a winter camp. "The little children eat and amuse themselves from morning to night," marveled Point. "Strangely, they never seem to quarrel."

In camp after the hunt, women begin the task of butchering a buffalo carcass. "The men sleep while the women dry the meat and dress the hides," observed Point. The hides, he noted, went for clothing and shelter. "A single lodge sometimes requires 15 or 20 hides."

LIFE IN CAMP

"We camped in a
spot where the
kingdom of nature
offered all the very
best to fulfill
our needs."

"Since these hunts were long affairs," observed Point, "the hunters took with them everything they possessed." Above, an interior view of a chief's lodge shows the layout of a high-ranking household. At left, an evening camp is being erected. Most of these duties fell to the women, who could set up the family lodge in roughly 15 minutes after a hard day's travel.

THE ART OF WARFARE

"The nomadic life of our
neophytes was not without
its attractions. But it was full
of perils because it took them
into enemy territory. . ."

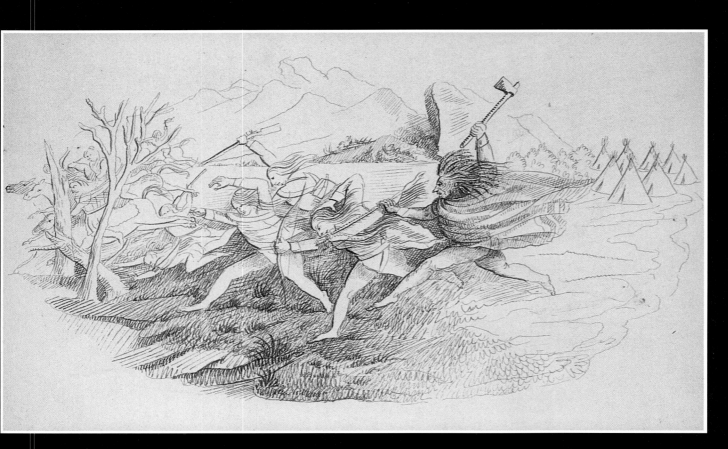

*A Flathead warrior known as the Thunderer, hatchet raised and face
ablaze with painted war medicine, attacks a party of Blackfeet
outside a hunting camp. Plateau tribes in search of buffalo faced constant
danger from the Plains peoples on whose lands the animals grazed.*

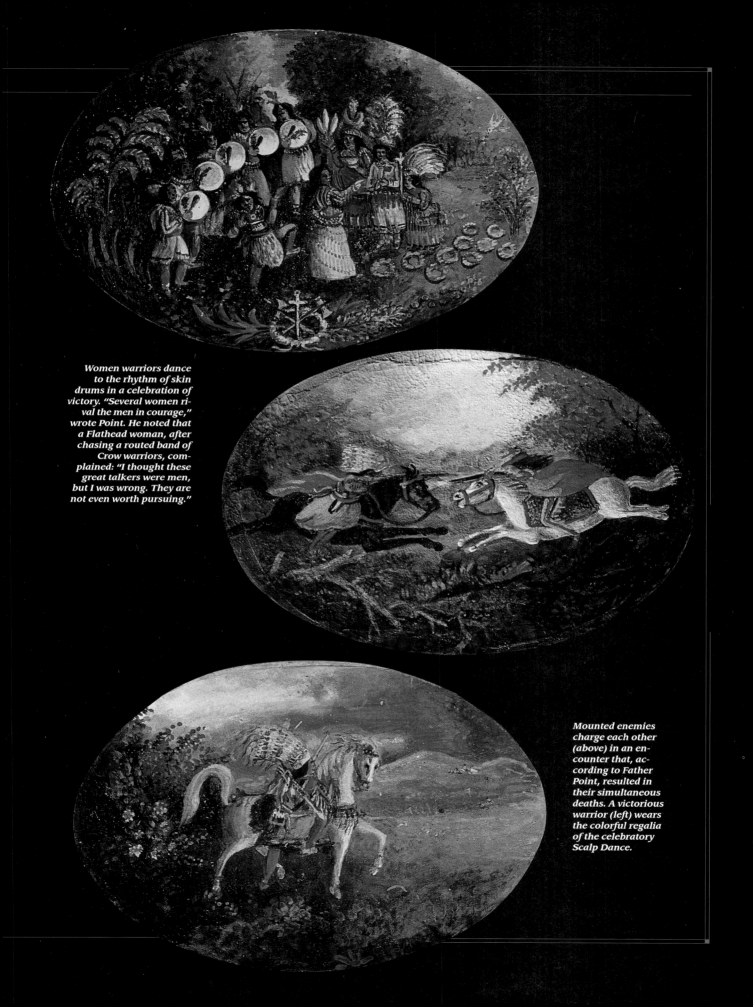

Women warriors dance to the rhythm of skin drums in a celebration of victory. "Several women rival the men in courage," wrote Point. He noted that a Flathead woman, after chasing a routed band of Crow warriors, complained: "I thought these great talkers were men, but I was wrong. They are not even worth pursuing."

Mounted enemies charge each other (above) in an encounter that, according to Father Point, resulted in their simultaneous deaths. A victorious warrior (left) wears the colorful regalia of the celebratory Scalp Dance.

MAGIC AND MEDICINE

A medicine man calls for help from the traditional spirits, or manitous, in this ceremony captured by Father Point's brush. A zealous missionary, Point had little patience with the native religion of his flock.

"They called 'manitou' that is, 'spirit' such apparently animated objects as the sun, thunder, and so forth, and the cult they practiced they called medicine."

A medicine man (above) and a "sorcerer" (left) display otherworldly powers while performing the rituals of their offices. Although the Indians embraced the aspects of Catholicism that they found useful, traditional religious practice continued despite the protestations of the missionaries.

Medecine d'Ignace

Ignace, a Coeur d'Alene chief, prays for the animal spirits of the forest in order to receive good hunting medicine. The guardian spirits bestowed a powerful vision on an applicant only after he underwent a solitary pilgrimage followed by ritual sweating and fasting.

Saint Mary's among the Flatheads, the mission that Father Point helped establish, celebrates its first sacrament of baptism on December 3, 1841. Point's Latin inscription framing the Indian gathering reads, "Thou shalt cleanse me and I shall be made whiter than snow."

3

IN DEFENSE OF THE HOMELAND

White River Utes, facing further white encroachment on their already reduced territory, pose with their firearms for an 1870s photo in Colorado Springs. Chief Colorow, front right, was one of many western range leaders willing to fight for their homelands.

Each spring Northern Paiutes journeyed to a miraculous expanse of water located in the parched scrubland of western Nevada to share in its remarkable bounty. By April the shores of this lake were teeming with ducks, geese, pelicans, and other migratory birds that offered welcome sustenance to the people after the long hard winter. The deep waters yielded even greater rewards a short time later when swarms of fish—cutthroat trout up to two feet long and the smaller but plentiful suckers called cui-ui—surged from the lake into the river that fed it and raced upstream to spawn amid the snowcapped Sierras to the west. Paiutes called the local band that hosted the spring gathering here the Cuyuiticutta, or Cui-ui Eaters. Yet the blessings that came from the waters belonged to no one group. By tradition, local Paiutes were obliged to welcome neighboring bands to these prime foraging grounds. Indeed, the spring assembly was a time for the Numa, or People, as Paiutes referred to themselves, to renew the ties of kinship and courtesy that brought them peace and a measure of prosperity in a land of limited resources.

When white men first approached the lake, Indians greeted them in the spirit of hospitality that had long prevailed there. In 1844 the explorer John Charles Frémont, leading a party down from Oregon east of the Sierras, came upon a remarkable "sheet of green water, some 20 miles broad," and dubbed it Pyramid Lake for a cone of volcanic tuff rising some 300 feet from the water's eastern edge. There Frémont met with the Cuyuiticutta, who invited his party to camp by the lake and shared fish with the visitors. Among the Indians Frémont befriended in the area was a local leader he called Captain Truckee, a Paiute word meaning "good" that the Indians used to greet their guests. That same name was conferred on the sparkling waterway that fed Pyramid Lake—the Truckee River, which emanated from Lake Tahoe high in the Sierras.

For a time, Indians around Pyramid Lake remained kindly disposed to whites. Captain Truckee and some of his followers accompanied Frémont to California in 1846 and aided him in the successful American campaign

to wrest control of that territory from the Mexicans. In later years, Captain Truckee urged his people to remain on good terms with the Americans and even encouraged them to salute the United States flag. Although his band was only one among several in the area, he had family ties to other Northern Paiute leaders, and whites saw him as a powerful ally.

American officials trusted that Captain Truckee's son-in-law and eventual successor, Winnemucca, would prove to be equally friendly and influential. In 1859 Indian agent Frederick Dodge optimistically touted Winnemucca as chief of the Northern Paiutes. As a matter of fact, the tribe's various bands remained autonomous, and their leaders were better described as headmen, or camp advisers, than as chiefs. Furthermore, Winnemucca harbored growing doubts about the Americans. For some time, he had looked on anxiously as emigrants sliced their way through Paiute territory on the California Trail. Now thousands of miners were pouring in to exploit the newly discovered silver deposits of the Comstock Lode in western Nevada. The patience of Winnemucca and his fellow leaders was beginning to wear thin. Like tribal chiefs all across the western range, they had reason to doubt that the oncoming multitudes would honor the generous spirit of the land and share equitably in its gifts.

The clear waters of Pyramid Lake—named for the natural stone prominence rising just left of center in this photograph—extend for 30 miles in northwestern Nevada. Paiutes guarded the lake jealously because its fish were crucial to their survival.

In the spring of 1860, Winnemucca's band joined others at Pyramid Lake as they had done so often in the past. On this occasion, however, the people had more on their minds than fishing. At night, leaders of the assembled bands, including some Bannocks and Shoshones with kinship ties to the Paiutes, made their way from separate camps to meet around a common council fire. At issue was a matter of great urgency—whether to wage war against the whites.

This debate posed a dilemma for leaders who had been close to Captain Truckee and adhered to his policy of accommodation—including Winnemucca and his nephew Numaga, whom the Indians looked to as their war leader. For Winnemucca and Numaga, going to war meant defying men they considered friends, among them Major William Ormsby, a businessman and militia commander in the territorial capital of Carson City, south of Pyramid Lake. As a favor, Ormsby had earlier invited Winnemucca's daughters, Sarah and Elma, to live with his family for a while so that they could learn English and the ways of white people. (The girls were later enrolled in a Catholic boarding school in California, but they were sent home after a few weeks when the parents of white students there objected to their daughters' mingling with Indians on equal terms.)

Few others around the council fire at Pyramid Lake felt much affection for the white intruders. In the past year, they had seen their homeland besieged by heedless strangers who cut down the nut-laden piñon trees for fuel and timber; diverted precious spawning streams and fouled the waters with runoff from mining operations; or set their cattle to roam on scarce pastures grazed by herds of ponies acquired in recent years by the once horseless Paiutes. With their subsistence patterns disrupted, the Paiutes had suffered through an unusually hungry winter, prompting some bands to raid white settlements for food or to prey on livestock. Antagonized by such incursions—and by murders and other misdeeds that were blamed on local Indians with little or no proof—settlers had begun arming for conflict with the Paiutes.

One spokesman after another rose at Pyramid Lake to recite their grievances and call for war. Winnemucca listened quietly without committing himself, although many there believed he was ready to defy the whites. The only one to speak out against war was the war leader himself, Numaga. Some thought him too friendly with whites: He could speak their language and had worked with them recently to avert conflict. But Paiutes would not have honored him as war leader if they doubted his courage. As a journalist described him a short time later, he was about 30 years old, six feet tall, and "straight as an arrow, with a depth and breadth of chest which denote great physical strength, and a quiet dignity and self-possession of manner which stamped him as a superior man."

Fully aware of the military power of the white men, Numaga argued that fighting them would be suicidal. His dissent forced the others to postpone a decision until unanimity could be achieved. Numaga then demonstrated his conviction by undergoing a painful ordeal. He stretched out on the ground outside his hut for three days and nights, with his face to the earth and his arms and legs extended, refusing all water and food despite entreaties from loved ones and protests from the other leaders. He meant to show them the error of their ways, even if it killed him.

On the fourth day, he heard voices from the nearby council circle chanting for war. He struggled to his feet, staggered over to the fire, and offered one last plea for peace—a speech that would live on in legend. The white men, he warned his listeners, were as numerous as the stars above: "You have wrongs, great wrongs, that rise up like those mountains before you; but can you, from the mountaintops, reach and blot out those stars?" Armed resistance, he added, would only condemn the Indians to a bitter exile: "You will be forced among the barren rocks of the north, where your ponies will die; where you will see the women and old men starve, and listen to the cries of your children for food. I love my people; let them live."

Northern Paiute war chief Numaga is seen above at age 30 in 1860, the year his warriors ambushed and destroyed a white militia led by the hapless Major William Ormsby (right), near the shore of Pyramid Lake. Numaga's devastation of Ormsby's better-armed but untrained volunteers has been described as a "bloody rabbit drive."

Numaga's speech had a marked effect on his listeners. But any lingering hope for peace was dashed when a rider came galloping up to the council circle with fateful news. Two 12-year-old Paiute girls had recently disappeared while foraging for roots, raising fears among their kin, who knew that white men in the area sometimes abducted Indian girls and raped them or sold them as slaves. A short time afterward, a Paiute reported hearing cries of distress emanating from Williams Station, a whiskey shop, trading post,

In this 1860s lithograph, soldiers drill on the parade ground of Fort Churchill, built after the Pyramid Lake War. From here on March 17, 1865, Nevada volunteer cavalrymen staged their raid on the Paiute Mud Lake camp in the dead of night, killing every man, woman, and child they could find, among them relatives of Chief Winnemucca.

and pony express stop on the Carson River south of Pyramid Lake. In response, a party of warriors—including the girls' father and Winnemucca's son Natchez—descended on the station and found the two girls tied with rags in the cellar. The angry warriors killed several white men on the premises and left Williams Station in flames.

Numaga, who had been attempting to coax his people back from the brink of war, realized now that he had no choice but to lead them forward against whites who were sure to seek retribution for the Indian attack. He abandoned his search for peace and assumed his task as war leader. He could command up to 1,000 fighting men—mostly Northern Paiutes, along with some Bannocks and Shoshones. He sent the women, children, and elders to seek shelter in the Black Rock Desert to the north. Then he deployed his warriors south of Pyramid Lake to meet the anticipated assault.

When the whites approached on May 12, they numbered only 105 men—raw volunteers from Carson City, Virginia City, and other settlements. Their horses were in poor condition for campaigning, but they were well armed with rifles and pistols, while most of the Indians carried only bows and arrows. Although led by Winnemucca's old friend, Major Ormsby, the volunteers harbored a contempt for the Paiutes that left no room for reconciliation. Riding along the Truckee River toward Pyramid Lake, they dreamed of vengeance and booty and sent up a crude war cry: "An Indian for breakfast and a pony to ride."

Numaga lured them toward the south shore of Pyramid Lake, where the Truckee streamed in through a broad meadow. Small parties of warriors appeared in the distance and drew the volunteers onward; then they vanished into the sagebrush. Numaga himself waited on his pony on top of a ridge that flanked the river to the east, holding an elaborate, two-headed peace pipe and battle-ax. As Ormsby and his men advanced along the river, they spotted Numaga on the ridge top, surrounded by 100 or so mounted warriors. Rising to the bait, Ormsby led a charge up the long slope toward the waiting Paiutes. As Numaga had anticipated, the uphill gallop tired the enemy horses, some of which faltered or turned back. Ormsby and those of his followers who made it to the brow of the ridge found that Numaga and his warriors had retreated into the distance. The attackers blundered ahead, and the trap was sprung. At every side, Indians emerged from behind clumps of sagebrush and rained arrows and bullets on their startled opponents.

Many volunteers fell in the furious barrage. The survivors milled about in a frenzy, trying to find a way out. Ormsby ordered them to fall back down the slope, but Numaga had posted a large group of warriors to their rear to cut off the escape route south. Indians on foot and on horseback closed in on the stranded volunteers, hurling them to the ground and slashing at them with their own swords. A few of Ormsby's men found gaps in the net Numaga was closing around them and escaped; others leaped into the river in the hope of reaching the far side, but drowned.

Numaga saw that the enemy was beaten and rode across the battlefield trying to put an end to the slaughter. In the frenzy of victory, however, his warriors fought on. According to one account, Numaga spotted Ormsby in the distance, dismounted and disoriented, and made an attempt to save his life. But an eager warrior dashed ahead of Numaga and brought the major down with arrows to his stomach and face. Ormsby was one of more than 60 men of the assault force to die that day.

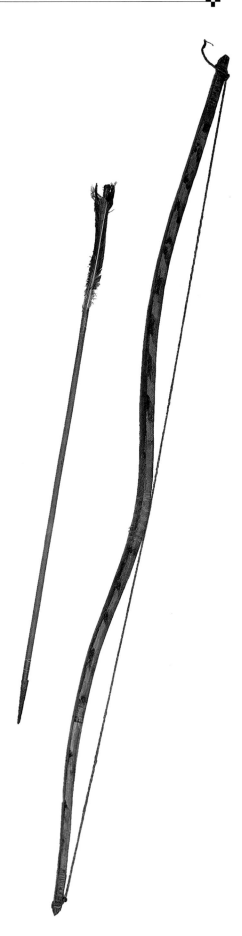

Southern Paiutes at Kanab, Utah, wear un-likely headdresses and fringed buckskin shirts that photographer John Hillers provid-ed as props for this 1873 picture. The weap-ons they hold are authentic—and well craft-ed like the Ute bow and arrow at left—but they were little match for white men's rifles.

News of Numaga's stunning vic-tory, carried by survivors straggling back from Pyramid Lake, spread panic along the Nevada-California border. Travel on the California Trail was disrupted, work on the Com-stock Lode stopped, and settlers be-gan fortifying their towns in antici-pation of Indian attacks. Pleas for help dispatched by telegraph to Cali-fornia brought a torrent of volun-teers and militia along with 200 U.S. Army regulars to stem the expected onslaught of Paiutes.

On the first of June, a column of avengers once again marched up the Truckee toward the lake. This time they numbered more than 800 men, and unlike Ormsby's volunteers, they were well disciplined and alert for ambush. On June 2, a furious battle erupted around the previous battle-ground, which rain and runoff had turned into a quagmire. For hours the Indians clung to the high ground, but they lost dozens of men and had to pull back that night. In the after-math, soldiers found the Paiute camps along the lake deserted. Nu-maga had led his followers north into the Black Rock Desert. There, as he had warned around the council fire, his people faced hunger and calamity "among the barren rocks." It was an ordeal few Paiutes would soon forget. Decades later, elders would recall how soldiers stationed near Pyramid Lake sent out messengers promising food and clothing to bands that came in of their own accord—and how one group that responded was mercilessly attacked. "Instead of getting bread and butter," a Paiute recollected, "they were getting bullets."

Numaga knew that the Paiutes would continue to pay a steep price for their rebellion against the government unless he came to terms with his formidable opponents. That the army was intent on crushing Paiute resistance was made clear in July, when soldiers constructed an adobe stronghold, Fort Churchill, along the Carson River near the burned-out remains of Williams Station, where the trouble had originated. In August Numaga received a visit in the desert from an army engineer, Colonel Frederick Lander, who made contact with the Paiutes unarmed, accompanied by only an interpreter. Lander explained that he had no authority to make commitments for his superiors but that he would urge them to deal fairly with the Paiutes if Numaga offered peace. The war leader replied that he was "glad, at last, to see a white man who comes to talk without promises." He agreed to an informal truce.

In the months ahead, Paiutes left their bleak desert hideouts and tried to pick up where they had left off. But settlers harried them, and officials offered them only vague promises that they could keep the land around Pyramid Lake as a reservation. Shortly before the conflict, Indian agent Dodge had proposed setting that area aside for the Northern Paiutes. But creation of the reservation would not be formally confirmed until an executive order was issued in 1874. In the meantime, white farmers and ranch-

SHOWTIME FOR A "PRINCESS"

As the portrait at near right indicates, Sarah Winnemucca usually dressed like young white women of the 1870s.

Her Paiute name was Thocmetony—"shellflower." But when her father, Chief Winnemucca, sent the child to live with whites to learn their ways, she acquired a white name: Sarah. From that time on, she lived in both worlds.

In 1864, trying to raise funds for their impoverished tribe, Sarah and her father and sister appeared onstage in a series of tableaux, contrived scenes with titles such as "The War Council" and "The Scalp Dance." The show yielded the family little income, but it helped prepare Sarah for the lecture circuit 15 years later. Her talks—in flawless English that surprised audiences—were insightful, humorous, and moving, and won her the respect of influential whites who could help the Indian cause.

ers appropriated prime land along the Truckee River and began diverting its flow, and the Central Pacific Railroad claimed the southern tip of the reserve for the transcontinental route whose construction would soon bring even more outsiders to the area.

Numaga and some 600 Paiutes remained around Pyramid Lake after the conflict in a kind of legal limbo. The former war leader welcomed government offers to teach his people to farm so that they could subsist there as whites encroached on their resources. But as he waited in vain for the federals to make good on the pledges, his people suffered. One measure of Paiute desperation was the decision of Old Winnemucca, as he was sometimes called, to appear onstage with his daughters in 1864 to raise money for food and blankets for their people. Together, the three performed tribal dances and scenes of Indian life at theaters in Virginia City and San Francisco. Young Sarah Winnemucca, who would later apply her skills as an orator to bring attention to the plight of the Paiutes, confided to a reporter that unnamed tribes had recently urged her father to join in a new war, but that as a longtime friend of the whites, he had refused.

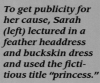

To get publicity for her cause, Sarah (left) lectured in a feather headdress and buckskin dress and used the fictitious title "princess."

Wearing an eclectic outfit, Chief Winnemucca assumes a Napoleonic pose on this visiting card from the 1860s.

The stage appearances proved to be less profitable than Old Winnemucca had hoped, and he returned to live with his band near Pyramid Lake. There he learned to his sorrow that the Paiutes were not safe from assault even within the limits of the proposed reservation. In March 1865, while he and the young men were off hunting antelope, a troop of cavalry searching for cattle thieves surrounded his band's encampment and attacked in the night without warning, gunning down old men, women, and children. Among the nearly 30 people killed were several of Winnemucca's close kin. Devastated, he abandoned his homeland and fled northward with a number of the survivors.

His nephew Numaga stayed on at Pyramid Lake, waiting in vain for the government to transform it into a workable reservation. He died there in 1871 of tuberculosis—one of many ailments that were introduced into the Indian population by the oncoming Americans, who had bequeathed little else to a people who once greeted them with gifts and good words.

Testament to the destructive encroachment of the whites, mountainous mounds of waste from silver mines tower above two domed Paiute dwellings at Virginia City in the 1860s.

The Pyramid Lake War and its melancholy aftermath epitomized the conflicts that swept like wildfires across the western range during this era of massive white encroachment. In western Nevada alone during the decade after Numaga's people waged their brief war, 287 Indians and 30 whites died in hostile encounters large and small. Although the events that triggered such violence varied from place to place, the underlying cause was relentless competition between the newcomers—who drew up boundaries and claimed the land and its resources as their inviolable property—and native peoples whose way of life depended on unrestricted movement across wide areas and free access to their ancestral hunting, fishing, and harvesting grounds.

Federal authorities often tried to resolve matters by confining tribes to reservations. As Indian agent Luther Mann put it crudely, "Wild Indians, like wild horses, must be corralled." Many Indians across the region fiercely opposed being corralled and moved onto reservations only under duress. Even when a tribe agreed to go peacefully, subsequent government actions frequently brought discord and violence. Government agents who administered the reservations were often incompetent or corrupt. And time after time, white settlers infringed on those tribal enclaves and pressured the government to break its own treaties and pare down the area that had been reserved for Indians.

By the time Numaga died at Pyramid Lake, many other tribal leaders of the western range had bravely resisted encroachment or confinement, only to meet with crushing setbacks. In 1871 a federal Indian agent encountered one such veteran, an old chief named Kamiakin, who was living in poverty and obscurity with a small band of his fellow Yakimas on a reservation in eastern Washington State. There was little fight left in the old war leader, observed the agent: "He is peaceable, but does not go much among the whites, and seems brokenhearted, having lost his former energy." Yet this desolate figure had at one time inspired diverse tribes to join in one of the broadest and boldest campaigns of defiance ever mounted against white authorities on the Plateau.

The origins of Kamiakin's uprising went back to the spring of 1855, when representatives of the United States government convened an enormous council in the Walla Walla Valley attended by 5,000 Indians from five different tribes. The site was only six miles from the charred remains of the Whitman mission, which Cayuse warriors had attacked in 1847 to dispel what they saw as the evil medicine of the white men. Many Indians at the Walla Walla council would soon conclude that the oncoming settlers were

In a display of tribal panoply, some 2,500 mounted Nez Percés sweep onto the site of the 1855 Walla Walla council. Governor Isaac I. Stevens (opposite, top) of Washington Territory appointed Lawyer (opposite, bottom)—a minor Nez Percé leader so named for his agile tongue—to be the tribe's chief negotiator. The sketches on these and the following two pages were made by an army artist, Private Gustavus Sohon.

more dangerous than ever and would have to be expelled from the land.

The main government spokesman there was Isaac I. Stevens, the brash young governor of the recently organized Washington Territory, which then extended eastward through what is now northern Idaho. A staunch advocate of settlement, Stevens was out to confine the native peoples living in Washington and the Oregon border country to reservations so that he could open the bulk of the territory to white farmers and ranchers. For days on end, he alternately threatened tribal chiefs and enticed them with promises of annuities and gifts. They would do well to accept such inducements, another official told them, since whites would descend "like grasshoppers on the plains. You cannot stop them."

At last, the majority of the chiefs were either won over or worn out and signed treaties that provided for three reservations: one for the Nez Percé; one for the Cayuse, Umatilla, and Wallawalla; and one for the Yakima and six other tribes that were not even represented at the council. In return, the tribes relinquished more than 60,000 square miles while retaining land that covered scarcely one-tenth that area. The ceded territory was to be the "Great Father's," as Stevens referred to the president, "for his white children."

After Stevens headed east to negotiate similar deals with the Spokane, Flatheads, and others, chiefs who had signed the Walla Walla treaties came to regret it. Stevens had assured them that they would have time to prepare their people for the changes to come. The treaties could not be enforced until ratified by the U.S. Senate, a process that Stevens had estimated would take two or three years and that in fact took four years. Less than two weeks after the council disbanded, however, word spread that Stevens had proclaimed all Indian land in the region between the Cascades and the Rockies open for settlement except those areas designated for the three reservations. Then, as if in response to Stevens's premature announcement, gold was discovered near Fort Colville, a trading post on the Columbia River near the Canadian border. Hordes of prospectors headed up the river from the coast or trekked through passes in the Cascades. Their journey took them through the heart of Yakima territory, and that tribe's principal chief, Kamiakin, emerged as the leading opponent of the treaties.

Kamiakin was a tall, strongly built man about 40 with a flair for oratory and kinship bonds to the chiefs of other tribes, including the Nez Percé,

Governor Stevens, in the midst of conference participants, exhorts the Indians to come to terms and yield territory to the government.

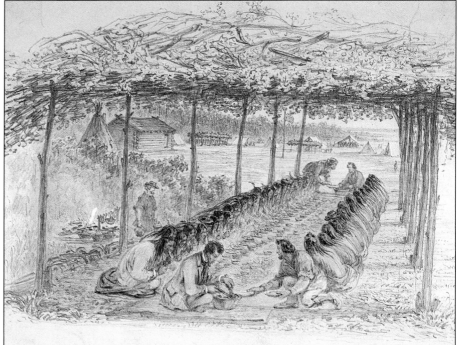

On the day after the Nez Percés arrived, Stevens and fellow treaty commissioner, Joel Palmer, join the tribe's chiefs for dinner, eating on tin plates beneath an arbor. It was the only time during the council they dined with the Indians.

Klickitat, and Spokane. He had attended Stevens's council and signed only reluctantly. Afterward he used his influence and powers of persuasion to call for an alliance against the intruding whites. "If they take our lands," he reportedly vowed, "their trails will be marked with blood!"

The conflict began on Kamiakin's home ground. He posted sentries at the passes in the Cascades to warn whites against entering Yakima territory, but some of them ignored the advice and thereby incurred the wrath of young men roused by Kamiakin's defiant words. In September 1855, three months after the Walla Walla conference, a group of five white men traveling along the Yakima River were killed in an assault led by a warrior by the name of Qualchin, who was a relative of Kamiakin's wife and the son of Chief Owhi, leader of a Yakima band called the Kittitas. Qualchin's deed impelled the reluctant Chief Owhi to pledge support to Kamiakin. Soon afterward, other whites in the area were attacked, prompting A. J. Bolon, the Indian agent to the Yakima, to cross over from the coast to investigate. He was waylaid by warriors who slit his throat and burned the body. Kamiakin prepared his forces for the armed confrontation that he knew was sure to follow.

Closing the council with the Scalp Dance, Nez Percé warriors sing of triumphs, while a woman insults an enemy's scalp that she twirls on a stick.

They were ready in early October when a column of 100 federal troops marched into Yakima country to teach Kamiakin a lesson. Five hundred Yakima warriors surprised the federals and drove them back south to Fort Dalles on the Columbia River. The bluecoats lost five soldiers in the rout and left behind their howitzer and packtrain in their haste.

Kamiakin's victory encouraged tribes on both sides of the Cascades to resist the intruders. As one Indian agent on the Plateau warned, "The volcano is about ready to break forth." In the months to come, a group of Yakimas crossed the Cascades to join coastal tribes in an attack on the infant settlement of Seattle, only to be driven off by gunfire from ships in the harbor. To the east, meanwhile, an expedition of more than 700 army regulars and volunteers had entered Yakima territory with the purpose of challenging Kamiakin's forces. When the chief made a peace overture through a Catholic missionary, the federal commander, Major Gabriel Rains, refused, vowing to "war forever until not a Yakima breathes in the land he calls his own." After some skirmishing, however, Major Rains withdrew with his forces for the winter to Fort Dalles, where at least one subordinate pronounced his expedition a total failure.

Elsewhere, tribes that remained uncertain about joining the resistance had the issue settled for them by a provocative contingent of 500 Oregon volunteers, who pushed east along the Oregon-Washington border, stirring up antagonism among Wallawallas, Cayuses, Umatillas, and Palouses. In early December, the Wallawalla chief, Peopeomoxmox—who had long been friendly to whites but was troubled by the proposed reservation—met the Oregon volunteers with a white flag and a request for a parley. The troops seized the chief and several of his companions as hostages and later killed them when their angry followers attacked. Although the campaign only increased tribal hostility toward whites, the returning volunteers proudly displayed the chief's severed ears, fingers, and scalp to settlers as trophies of victory.

Fighting persisted for the next year and then subsided, only to resume in the spring of 1858. The army, to Governor Stevens's dismay, had banned settlers from Indian country until the 1855 treaties were ratified. But prospectors heading for Colville were still permitted to cross tribal lands. Those incursions, together with a fresh government plan for an east-west road across the Plateau, provoked renewed calls by Kamiakin for allied resistance. In May 1858, an army column of 164 men bound for the troubled Colville district was assailed by several hundred warriors, including local Spokanes and Palouses along with allied Yakimas and Coeur d'Alenes. The beleaguered troops held out on a hilltop for a while, but they suffered many casualties and expended much of their ammunition and had to retreat in the night. Once again, soldiers fled from defiant Indians in such haste that they left behind their howitzers. Army commanders suspected that Kamiakin was responsible for the attack and swore never to negotiate with him or with any tribe abetting him.

In the ensuing conflict, known as the Coeur d'Alene War, the majority of the tribes living near what is now the Washington-Idaho border joined with Kamiakin's Yakimas in opposing the whites. The conspicuous holdouts were the Nez Percés, whose territory lay safely outside the miners'

In the late 1850s, the verdant Spokane Valley—photographed here by Edward Curtis years later—was the focus of bloody struggle for Indians who rejected the 1855 treaties.

paths and whose proposed reservation was the most generous of the three that had been negotiated at Walla Walla. Some Nez Percé chiefs remained skeptical of that deal, but others pledged friendship to the United States and even went so far as to furnish scouts for the army—derided by the defiant Indians as "soldiers' slaves."

This time the army moved against the Plateau insurgents with devastating effectiveness. Colonel George Wright swept into Spokane country

with a 400-mule packtrain and 700 soldiers, led by 30 Nez Percé scouts in new army uniforms. His men were well trained and equipped with howitzers and long-range rifles that "can reach the enemy," Wright wrote, "where he cannot reach us." In two battles near present-day Spokane in early September, Wright brought all these assets to bear against his allied opponents—including Coeur d'Alenes, Palouses, Spokanes, Yakimas, and Kalispels—and drove them from the cover of timber onto clear ground. Thus exposed, as many as 100 of the 500 or so warriors arrayed against the federals died in the two encounters. Wright's force emerged virtually unscathed, reporting a single soldier wounded.

The twin defeats snuffed out the flame of resistance, and Wright did all he could to ensure that it would never revive. Rejecting peace overtures from his vanquished foes, he led troops through their homelands, burning

In a drawing by Gustavus Sohon portraying the conflict on the Spokane plain in 1858, Chief Kamiakin's Yakimas and their allies have set grass fires in an attempt to repel the troops led by Colonel George Wright. The tactic failed; the mounted soldiers charged through the smoke and scattered the force of warriors, sending them to defeat.

lodges and stores of food, slaughtering 700 Palouse horses, and hanging 15 Indians deemed guilty of crimes against whites. Among those executed was Kamiakin's confederate, Qualchin, whom Wright captured by first detaining his father, Chief Owhi, and threatening the old man with death until he sent for his son. After Qualchin was hanged, the grieving Owhi seized a horsewhip, struck the lieutenant who was guarding him, and tried to escape, only to be shot dead in the attempt. Kamiakin, for his part, managed to avoid capture by fleeing northward. As a defeated war leader, he was later allowed by the federals to rejoin his people and live out his days on the reservation he had so stoutly resisted.

The struggle was over for Kamiakin and his allies. But for the Nez Percés, who had declined to join them, a bitter confrontation lay ahead. In 1877, just a few months after Kamiakin's death, members of that tribe found themselves embroiled in their own conflict with the Americans. Some Nez Percés liked to boast that they had never harmed the whites. But relations had deteriorated since the Nez Percés were promised a large reservation in 1855. After the discovery of gold there in 1860, the federal government proposed cutting the reservation to one-tenth its original size and won the assent of tribal leaders living in the reduced area, along the Clearwater River in western Idaho. Those leaders signed a new treaty in 1863, but chiefs of several bands to the south balked at signing and refused to move.

For many of the nontreaty Nez Percés, adhering to their homeland was a spiritual imperative. Like disaffected Indians in other parts of the region, they were inspired by defiant prophets, or dreamers, who rejected the white man's religion. Instead, the dreamers urged their followers to remain true to their native beliefs—in particular, their devotion to the land, referred to reverently as the Earth Mother, and to the Great Spirit above. If Indians kept faith with those powers, dreamers prophesied, they would achieve redemption and be free forever from the baneful influence of the white man. Their hope was to "live as free and unrestricted as their fathers," observed Oregon's superintendent of Indian affairs. "They aspire to be Indians and nothing else."

Although badly wounded, Kamiakin escaped to Canada after the Spokane setback, slipping back into his homeland in 1861. Once so rich that he reportedly owned 1,000 horses, he lived in poverty until his death in 1877.

"The reservation is too small for so many people," pleaded Chief Joseph (left) when the government moved to reduce Nez Percé territory by nine-tenths. In the sketch above, another Nez Percé leader, Toohoolhoolzote, threatened by General Oliver Howard (foreground), gestures angrily. "I am a man," he shouted, "and will not go! I will not leave my home!" Rather than report to the reservation, the Nez Percés fled to the Plains, where they had long pitched hunting camps (background).

Such convictions were forcefully expressed by a Nez Percé spokesman named Toohoolhoolzote in May 1877, when General Oliver Otis Howard summoned the defiant Indian leaders to Fort Lapwai on the Idaho reservation to persuade them to move there. Howard, a devout Christian who believed that he was helping the Nez Percés by exposing them to reservation life, grew so annoyed by Toohoolhoolzote's fervent arguments to the contrary that he told him at one point to "shut up," eliciting a stinging response. "Who are you," the spokesman demanded, "that you ask us to talk, and then tell me I shan't talk? Are you the Great Spirit? Did you make the world? Did you make the sun? Did you make the rivers to run for us to drink? Did you make the grass to grow? Did you make all these things, that you talk to us as though we were boys?" Howard could think of no better reply than to place Toohoolhoolzote under arrest for several days as a lesson to the others. He then closed the conference by handing the Nez Percés an ultimatum to either report to the reservation within a month or face attack.

As the deadline approached, the holdouts were about to give in and move to the reservation when an impulsive assault by a few young Nez Percés on white settlers in the area raised fears of retribution by the federals. Many Nez Percés fled eastward into the rugged Idaho canyon country rather than report to the reservation. Prominent among them were Toohoolhoolzote and the peace-loving Chief Joseph, whose people had clung devotedly to their native Wallowa Valley in northeastern Oregon. Troops went after the fugitives, and on June 17, a 99-man cavalry detachment caught up with them at White Bird Canyon on the Salmon River. A civilian scout fired on a Nez Percé party approaching under a white flag of truce. In the resulting battle, a group of 70 warriors armed with bows and arrows and old guns thoroughly outmaneuvered their opponents and killed 34 soldiers without losing a single man.

Stung by the outcome of the engagement, the army relentlessly pursued the elusive party of some 700 men, women, and children toward the Montana border and down along the Continental Divide. More than once, troops closed in on the Nez Percés and attacked, only to be driven off by warriors intent on shielding their families from harm. In August the fugitives crossed the divide at Targhee Pass and entered the recently established Yellowstone National Park. At the time of their arrival, agents there were working to transform that place into a haven for white visitors and would soon ban all Indians from the park. But for a short time, at least, Yellowstone belonged to the Nez Percés, who accosted a startled group of

tourists, held them hostage for several days to keep them from betraying the party's whereabouts, and insisted they trade their fresh horses, saddles, and guns for the fugitives' worn-out gear.

From Yellowstone, the Nez Percés proceeded northward into Montana, where they hoped to obtain assistance from Crow Indians who had been friendly to them in the recent past. Like other parties from the Plateau who had ventured onto the grasslands in earlier times, however, the Nez Percés met with grief there. In late September, army troops, aided by Crow scouts, surrounded them amid the rolling hills of northern Montana and brought their valiant struggle to an end with a punishing attack that claimed the lives of Toohoolhoolzote and many others. A small number of fugitives fled into Canada, but most of the survivors followed the lead of the heartsick Chief Joseph, who surrendered with about 400 cold and hungry survivors and pledged to "fight no more forever."

Chief Joseph's reluctant decision to surrender ensured the survival of his people. Shown here are his grandson Joe Redthunder (center) and Redthunder's sons and grandsons, surrounding him in this Father's Day photo in 1994.

Few other peoples of the western range who dreamed of maintaining the Indian way of life escaped similar retribution during this tragic period. Earlier, while the Civil War was still raging in the East, Northern Shoshones living along the Bear River in southern Idaho had attacked settlers and emigrants who were trespassing on their hunting and foraging grounds. In response, 300 California recruits under Colonel Patrick Connor trudged northward through the snow from Fort Douglas near Salt Lake City in January 1863 and surrounded the village of Chief Bear Hunter. There they clashed with opposing warriors and killed more than 250 Shoshones, including a number of women and children.

Survivors of that massacre were later confined with other Shoshones and Bannocks at the Fort Hall Reservation in southeastern Idaho, where they were promised regular rations and help in farming. At Fort Hall as elsewhere in the region, however, agriculture proved difficult, and government agents, through either dishonesty or incompetence, often failed to provide sufficient rations. To compensate, Indians continued to venture abroad from time to time to hunt and gather.

In the spring of 1878, a party from Fort Hall composed mainly of Bannocks joined with Northern Paiutes from the Malheur Reservation in southeastern Oregon to dig roots on the Camas Prairie, located midway between the two reservations. By treaty, this area was supposed to be a Bannock reservation, but it was never formally reserved as such. Meanwhile, hogs kept by white settlers were roaming the prairie and digging up the camas roots. Angry Indians from the two reservations first fought with some settlers they blamed for despoiling their land, then organized a war party of about 200 men that headed west into Oregon, clashing with whites along the way. Soon the warriors picked up fresh support from the Malheur Reservation. Among the leaders of the resistance movement were two determined Paiutes, a chief named Egan and a spiritual leader called Oytes, who saw it as his sacred duty to oppose the white men and their ways. He denounced any attempt at farming as an affront to the earth, "our mother," for example, and insisted that his followers live on "what grows of itself." He also believed that his medicine rendered him invulnerable to the white man's bullets.

The defiant Paiutes and Bannocks tried to secure the support of Old Winnemucca, who had settled at Malheur with his followers after the troubles around Pyramid Lake. According to his daughter Sarah—who opposed the uprising and offered her services to the army as an interpreter and scout—warriors detained her father while she was away and forced

him to leave the reservation with some of his kinsmen and join the hostile camp in the mountains nearby. Sarah told of sneaking into that camp a short time later and persuading her father to flee with his followers and place them under the army's protection. Those Paiutes and Bannocks who remained hostile were pursued by federal troops and ultimately sought sanctuary on the Umatilla Reservation in northern Oregon. Some Umatillas so resented their presence, however, that they killed Chief Egan and betrayed the whereabouts of Oytes and his followers to the army. A number of the Bannocks managed to escape eastward, only to be captured by troops near Yellowstone Park in September.

The last major war of resistance on the western range was waged the next year in Colorado by Utes who hoped to avoid the fate of their tribal counterparts in Utah. There settlers and troops had pressed all Ute bands in the territory onto the Uintah Reservation, a tract of some two million acres in northeastern Utah that Brigham Young himself characterized as a "vast contiguity of waste." In Colorado, Ute leaders tried to conclude a better deal with the federal government, but their efforts were complicated by fresh discoveries of gold, silver, and other precious ores. No sooner had Ute chiefs agreed in 1868 to accept a 15-million-acre reservation in western Colorado than rich new finds were reported in the San Juan Mountains on land set aside by treaty for the "absolute and undisturbed use" of the Indians. Fortune hunters flooded the area, and within a few years, federal negotiators were pressing the Utes for further concessions.

During the talks, officials paid special regard to a shrewd and accommodating chief by the name of Ouray, who was the leader of the largest of several Ute bands in the territory—the Taviwach, or Uncompahgres, who ranged across west-central Colorado. Ouray's father had married a Jicarilla Apache in present-day New Mexico, where their son grew up in close contact with whites and learned to speak Spanish and English before coming of age in Colorado among his fellow Uncompahgres. Short, barrel-chested, and muscular, Ouray was a crack shot and adept with a knife, and he distinguished himself in forays with other men of his band on the plains of eastern Colorado, where they hunted buffalo and clashed with rivals such as the Comanches. Once he became chief, however, Ouray staunchly advocated peace with whites. His very name forecast his role as a conciliator: It came from a Ute term meaning "yes," which he was fond of saying to his parents as a baby.

Ouray played a prominent role in working out the treaty of 1868, and as a result, federal negotiators leaned heavily on him in their subsequent

Accompanied by a boy with an ornate shoulder bag, a Uintah Ute shows off his war regalia in 1874, six years before defeated Colorado Utes were forced to join their kinsmen in this desolate part of Utah.

attempts to amend that agreement and further reduce the size of the reservation. Ouray at first resisted their appeals. "We do not want to sell a foot of our land," he proclaimed on behalf of his fellow chiefs in 1872; "that is the opinion of all." At the same time, however, he recognized that the Utes were becoming increasingly dependent on the government. The plains where they had long stalked buffalo were being taken over by white hunters and cattle ranchers, and he concluded that it would not be long before the Utes would have little choice but to learn the ways of white men and subsist as farmers and herdsmen. To do so, he believed, they would have to remain on good terms with federal authorities, who retained the power to reward their friends and crush their foes.

Ouray was not averse to being personally rewarded for cooperating with the federals. He was already receiving $500 a year to act as an interpreter for the government. And when the negotiators tried once again to persuade the Utes to yield land in 1873, they promised Ouray an annual bonus of $1,000 for a pe-

Ute chief Ouray and wife Chipeta (above) are dressed in fancy clothes for a visit to Washington, D.C. Ouray wore this buckskin shirt (shown in detail at far right) for important tribal occasions.

riod of 10 years if he agreed to back the deal. In the end, he was able to prevail upon other chiefs to sign a new agreement that ceded to the United States nearly four million acres, or approximately one-fourth of the reservation, in return for annuities and hunting rights on the ceded land.

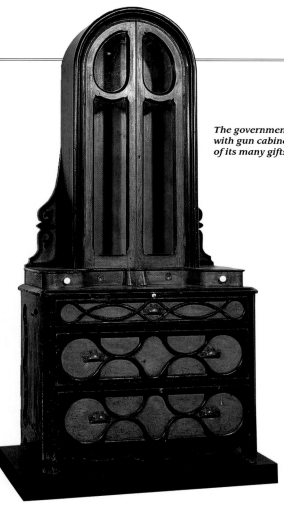

The government had this desk with gun cabinet made as one of its many gifts for Ouray.

Ouray's visiting card declares him "Chief of the Utes," a title bestowed by the government but without basis in tribal tradition.

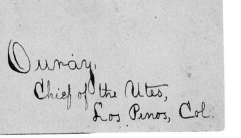

This concession did little to endear Ouray to those Utes who hoped to live as their ancestors had. Even before the most recent deal with the federals, some Utes had denounced Ouray for his accommodating stance and had tried to kill him. Moreover, he had further distanced himself from traditionalists by establishing a 160-acre homestead, where he raised sheep, hay, and vegetables and lived in an adobe house provided by the government and furnished by his wife with such amenities as curtains, carpets, a brass bed, and a silver tea service. Ouray proudly presented himself as "head chief" of the tribe, but not all Utes were inclined to heed his counsel or follow in his path.

Agitation mounted within the tribe as prospectors made new mineral strikes and crowded in on the reservation, clashing with Utes from time to time. In 1876, after Colorado attained statehood, citizens took up the rallying cry "The Utes must go!" Whites blamed the Indians for murders and other calamities, even holding them responsible for forest fires that struck during times of drought. Utes hoped that the government would protect them, but instead they found their traditions threatened by federal policies. Matters came to a head at the White River Agency, which served two bands that occupied territory north of Ouray's Uncompahgres. There in the spring of 1878, Indian agent Nathan Cook Meeker—an eccentric 61-year-old former storekeeper, poet, newspaper correspondent, and social visionary who had helped found the utopian community of Greeley north of Denver—embarked on a campaign to transform proud hunter-gatherers into farmers virtually overnight. When the White River Utes balked, Meeker treated them like naughty children, withholding supplies due them under the treaty and trying to keep them from hunting beyond the reservation's boundaries.

Meeker even went so far as to fence off and plow up for farming choice pasture where local Utes had long grazed the ponies that were so important to their way of life. This move put him at odds with Ouray's brother-in-law, a medicine man named Johnson. Meeker had recently praised Johnson for raising cows and a bumper crop of potatoes. But Johnson was equally devoted to his horses and confronted the agent in his office on September 8, 1879. Meeker tried to brush him off. "You have too many ponies," he told Johnson. "You had better kill some of them." The powerfully built Johnson lifted Meeker bodily, carried him out to the porch, and threw him against the hitching rail.

Meeker was only bruised, but he dispatched urgent telegrams to his superiors demanding protection, and a detachment of 150 U.S. troops came down from Wyoming. Before reaching the reservation, they were met by a party of Utes from White River under a war leader named Jack. Chief Jack was fluent in English—he had been raised in Salt Lake City by

Ute Chief Captain JACK—of the Thornburg Massacre.

Chief Jack, also known as Green Leaf, led White River Ute warriors against federal troops in 1879. Many of the warriors were armed with Springfield army rifles like the one above.

Chief Douglas, attired in a suit for this portrait, mounted the attack that took the life of Indian agent Nathan Meeker and nine other white men in the Ute uprising of 1879.

Mormons who purchased him from Utes—and he asked the federal commander, Major Thomas Thornburgh, to proceed to the agency for talks with Ute leaders, accompanied by no more than five soldiers. Thornburgh agreed, but he later decided to bring his cavalry closer to the agency in case trouble arose. Reports of this movement convinced Chief Jack that the soldiers were coming to collar the Utes and drag them from their mountain homeland.

On September 29, when the federal column crossed Milk Creek, the northern boundary of the reservation, Chief Jack was waiting there with 100 well-armed warriors whom he had deployed on a ridge commanding the trail. Both sides waited, evidently hoping to avoid bloodshed. Then a federal officer stepped forward waving his hat as a token of peace, and someone—soldier or Ute—took it as another kind of signal and fired. Within minutes, Major Thornburgh fell dead with a bullet in the brain.

His troops pulled back to their supply train, and the Utes pressed the attack, raking the soldiers with gunfire and nearly smoking them out by igniting the prairie grass and sagebrush that surrounded them. Jack's Utes besieged the troops for several days. At least a dozen federals died in the fighting and many more were wounded, while the Utes suffered more than two dozen dead of their own. Finally, federal reinforcements arrived and broke the siege. Chief Jack and his warriors remained defiant, despite a message sent by Ouray through an Indian agent traveling under a white flag that "requested and commanded" the defiant Utes to cease hostilities against whites. By tribal custom, no leader could summarily command obedience, but Chief Jack was prepared to honor Ouray's request if the government authorities agreed to address the Utes' grievances.

The army declined to negotiate, however, and Jack and his men sought refuge in the mountains with other White River Utes led by a prominent chief named Douglas, whose followers had attacked the agency itself on September 29 after learning that soldiers had entered the reservation and were engaged in hostilities. That assault claimed the life of Nathan Meeker and nine other white men and destroyed the agent's headquarters along with plows, mowers, wagons, and other implements he had amassed to transform the Utes' way of life. When Chief Douglas and his followers took to the mountains, they brought with them as

MISS JOSEPHINE MEEKER, PHOTOGRAPHED BY BATE

THE UTE MASSACRE!
Brave Miss Meeker's Captivity!
HER OWN ACCOUNT OF IT.

ALSO,

The Narratives of Her Mother and Mrs. Price.

TO WHICH IS ADDED

FURTHER THRILLING AND INTENSELY INTERESTING DETAILS, NOT HITHERTO PUBLISHED, OF THE BRAVERY AND FRIGHTFUL SUFFERINGS ENDURED BY MRS. MEEKER, MRS. PRICE AND HER TWO CHILDREN, AND

BY MISS JOSEPHINE MEEKER.

PUBLISHED BY
THE OLD FRANKLIN PUBLISHING HOUSE,
PHILADELPHIA, PA.

Entered, according to Act of Congress, in the year 1879, by the OLD FRANKLIN Publishing House, in the office of the Librarian of Congress, at Washington, D. C.

hostages Meeker's wife and daughter Josephine and another white woman and her two children.

Newspaper accounts of white female hostages in the hands of Indians stirred up a frenzy. Some 1,500 government troops descended on the White River Agency, and thousands more stood ready to support them. In Washington, Secretary of the Interior Carl Schurz, fearing for the lives of the captives, authorized a one-man rescue mission and entrusted it to Charles Adams, a former Indian agent who had retained the confidence of the Utes. The first stop on Adams's journey was the reservation homestead of his old friend, Chief Ouray. As was his custom in times of trouble, Ouray had swapped his European-style clothing for traditional buckskins. But he was shaken by the uprising and debilitated by a worsening kidney ailment. Too weak to accompany Adams himself, the chief sent along a delegation of 13 Utes that was led by his brother-in-law Sapovanero.

Josephine Meeker (above, left), held hostage for 23 days by the White River Utes, wrote of her ordeal in a book whose title page appears above. Charges that she and other women captives were raped caused a stir but were never leveled in court.

The group quickly located the fugitives' mountain camp and confronted Chief Douglas, the resistance leader. He refused to release the hostages unless the troops stopped advancing against his camp; Adams refused to ask the army to halt until the hostages were freed. Sapovanero then issued Douglas and his followers an ultimatum from his ailing brother-in-law: Let the whites go, or Ouray himself would send warriors against the defiant Utes. Sensing his isolation, Douglas asked Adams if he truly had the power to keep the federal troops at bay. Adams replied that he was acting by authority of the president and that the army would surely listen to him. At that, Chief Douglas freed the three women and two children, thereby averting a deadly confrontation.

For the Utes, however, there was a steep price to pay. Troops remained at the White River Agency in force, and charges were pressed against Chief Douglas, Ouray's kinsman Johnson, and 10 other Utes for crimes related to the attack at the agency and the abduction of the women and children. (The 12 were never tried, but Chief Douglas was imprisoned at Fort Leavenworth, Kansas, for nearly a year before being released.) Meanwhile, Coloradans cited the uprising as reason for abolishing the reservation, which was one of the largest tracts of valuable Indian real estate remaining in the West. Ouray and other Ute leaders were summoned to Washington early in 1880 and prodded into selling the reservation—except for a strip of land in the extreme southwestern portion belonging to the Southern Ute bands—for about 12 cents an acre.

Under the provisions of the new treaty, the White River bands were removed westward to the desolate Uintah Reservation. Ouray's Uncompahgres were promised farms in fertile river valleys near present-day Grand Junction, Colorado, and the ailing chief persuaded his people that this was the best solution to their dilemma they could hope for. But scarcely a year after Ouray's death in August 1880, federal authorities broke their promise and forced the Uncompahgres at gunpoint onto a new reservation in Utah. Located just south of the Uintah, it was comparably barren. Only its name, the Ouray Reservation, recalled the green mountains and grand hopes that the chief had clung to in happier times.

Indians of the western range who endured the transition to reservation life faced a new challenge beginning in 1887 when the federal government instituted its allotment program. Under this policy, which was applied on a case-by-case basis over a period of several decades, land on many reservations around the region was removed from collective tribal ownership and allotted to Indian heads of families or single adults in parcels ranging from 40 to 640 acres.

The stated objective of the program was to encourage Indians to become independent farmers and ranchers. But its overriding effect was to further reduce tribal holdings. Population densities on most reservations in the region were quite low, and once the allotments were made, the large areas that remained unoccupied were sold off by the government to white homesteaders, ranchers, and prospectors. To make matters worse, some Indians who received allotments were unable to make a living on them and sold or rented their tracts at the first opportunity and moved away. This misconceived program helped shrink the 1.8-million-acre Fort Hall Reservation, which was home to about 1,200 Shoshones and Bannocks in the late 1800s, to less than one-third its original size. Over in western Montana, the Flathead Reservation—occupied not only by Flatheads but also by Kootenais, Kalispels, and others—was reduced in area by roughly a million acres.

Allotment hit the Nez Percés just as they were beginning to recover from the defeat of 1877. The fugitives who surrendered in Montana that year had been exiled to the Indian Territory of present-day Oklahoma, where they languished for several years. Chief Joseph and his Wallowa band were later sent to join members of several other tribes on the Colville Reservation in Washington State, but the other Nez Percé fugitives were allowed to settle on the tribe's reservation in Idaho in 1885. They arrived there on the Fourth of July, a holiday that the reservation dwellers had made their own by staging horse races, games of chance, dances, and other festivities associated with their traditional midyear camas harvest. Henceforth, the celebration had extra significance as the date when the cherished exiles returned to their homeland.

It would take more than a national holiday, however, to reconcile Nez Percés to the American way of life. When government authorities allotted their reservation in the 1890s, many were taken aback. "How is it that we have not been consulted in this matter?" demanded one elder. "This is our land by long possession and by treaty." Even some Indians who had converted to Christianity and were adopting the new ways of the white man were dismayed by the program. "We do not want our land cut up in little pieces," complained a Nez Percé who was serving as judge on a reservation tribunal. "We have not told you to do it."

In the end, however, the reservation dwellers saw nothing to be gained by resistance and went along with an allotment that resulted in

Lured by ads such as the one at right, home-steaders gather to claim land on Montana's Flathead Reservation. In 1906 each member of the Flathead tribe was granted an 80- to 160-acre plot, opening a "surplus" two-thirds of the reservation to white settlement.

the sale of a half-million acres of tribal land to homesteaders. The proceeds of the transaction went to the Nez Percés, but that brief boost in income scarcely compensated for the long-term damage to tribal morale, as white settlers and merchants hemmed in the Indians, sold them liquor, and snapped up more land when allotment holders were unable to make a go of it as farmers. The results confirmed the words of Chief Joseph, who had warned of the cost of parting with one's territory. "The earth and myself are of one mind," he insisted. "The measure of the land and the measure of our bodies are the same."

In the Great Basin, the divisive allotment program drove the White River Utes to one last act of resistance, albeit bloodless. In 1905 their Uintah Reservation was broken up into allotments of a mere 80 acres each. The remainder of the land was set aside for a national forest and for homesteaders. The following year, in a desperate attempt to secure territory that was free of intruders, several hundred White River Utes set off for South Dakota, where they hoped to struggle for a homeland with the assistance of the Lakota Sioux and other tribes that had been at odds with the government in recent times. In the end, they were escorted by troops back to their diminished reservation in Utah. There, unable to hunt and gather freely as they once had and ill equipped to prosper on small parcels of arid land as farmers

Northern Paiutes gather to receive an issue of tents and blankets from government agents in 1900. Such handouts rarely met the needs of the Indians. "A family numbering eight persons got two blankets," said Sarah Winnemucca after one distribution day. "It was the saddest affair I ever saw."

Reservation ration tickets like this one belonging to Chief Ouray were punched after each week's issue of staples. Such tickets were often kept in a hide pouch (left).

or ranchers, they became ever more dependent on government support.

Not all Indians of the region settled on conventional reservations. Some camped near frontier settlements or forts, performing menial tasks or fending off hunger by begging, scavenging, or resorting to prostitution. (The phrase for venereal disease in the Shoshone language was "black clothing sickness," a reference to the dark uniforms worn by the U.S. Cavalry.) Other Indians lived in so-called colonies, small reservation-like enclaves established by the federal government on farms or on the outskirts of towns. Regardless of their location, nearly all felt the anguish of being ripped loose from their cultural moorings.

As native peoples struggled through this time of collective trauma, many embraced homegrown religious movements in the hope of reclaiming the spiritual if not the earthly powers of their ancestors. Resistance leaders among the Nez Percé and other tribes had recently drawn inspiration from prophet-dreamers who told of a better day to come when Indians would be free of the white man. Few Indians still believed that they could achieve that goal through warfare. But some remained convinced that the spirits they prayed to would destroy the white man's world and ultimately unite them with their departed ancestors. Among the chief exponents of this dreamer faith on the Plateau was a short, hump-backed shaman by the name of Smohalla. Born into the tiny Wanapum tribe of eastern Washington about 1815, Smohalla and his prophecies were blamed by whites for helping to inspire such diverse conflicts as Kamiakin's uprising and the flight of the Nez Percés. But Smohalla continued to exert great influence in later years, at a time when armed resistance had been crushed and the Indians felt powerless.

Until the time of his death in 1895, Smohalla lived with his followers near Priest Rapids on the Columbia River, northwest of the Yakima Reservation. Overlooked by earlier treaty makers, the Wanapum managed to avoid confinement, and Smohalla's community remained a bastion of traditional values. There he staged rituals that attracted Yakimas and other Indians from surrounding areas. They met in a tule-mat longhouse on the banks of the Columbia and joined in rousing ceremonies meant to prepare them for the end of the world. Accompanied by the pounding of drums and ringing of bells, they danced and waved eagle and swan feathers that they believed would help them rise up on the day of reckoning and join their beloved ancestors in a better place.

Until that day arrived, Smohalla urged, the faithful were to avoid alien practices such as farming that violated the solemn bond between the people and their Earth Mother. He likened plowing the ground to tearing his mother's bosom with a knife and making hay to cutting her precious hair. So powerful was the appeal of those sentiments to his supporters that at least 200 Yakimas refused to accept allotments for farming when their reservation was divided up, at the risk of seeing the land sold off to whites. Well into the 20th century, many Indians in the area adhered to some version of the cult that was inspired by Smohalla.

To the south, a similar movement known as the Ghost Dance had blossomed amid the harsh conditions endured by Nevada's Paiutes. Like Smohalla's ritual, the Ghost Dance reinterpreted ancient religious traditions. For countless generations, Paiutes had thanked the spirits for the bounty they received and celebrated their communal bonds by singing and dancing in joyous circles. Then during the early days of the reservation period, a Northern Paiute shaman named Wodziwob taught his followers an apocalyptic new round dance that had appeared to him in a vision. Men, women, and children were to join in a circle, their fingers interlocked, and shuffle to the left while singing sacred songs. If they performed this dance for at least five nights in succession, he prophesied, the ghosts of their ancestors would be restored to life, and the world would be as it had been before the white man arrived.

This original Ghost Dance took hold among Wodziwob's followers on Nevada's Walker River Reservation about 1870 and spread quickly to other groups in the Great Basin and in parts of California and the Plateau. In most places, the initial enthusiasm soon died out when the prophecy went unfulfilled. But the movement was revived a generation later by the North-

Smohalla, facing the camera in white, sits cross-legged among his dreamer cult followers in the late 1880s. The deprivations of reservation life for Indians in the late 19th century fueled their interest in the apocalypse Smohalla prophesied—one that would reunite them with their departed kin.

ern Paiute medicine man Wovoka, renowned for his power to heal wounds, cure illnesses, and summon rain. His father had been a follower of Wodziwob, but the young Wovoka also absorbed elements of Christianity while working for a Presbyterian rancher named David Wilson, who gave him the name Jack Wilson. Wovoka was in his early thirties when the sun went into eclipse on January 1, 1889, and he experienced an apocalyptic vision. When "the sun died," he later explained, he too died and went to heaven, where he saw the dead "all happy and forever young." God then told him to return to earth and prepare his people for the new day to come, when they would be reunited with their departed kin and live with them in eternal harmony. Like Wodziwob, Wovoka urged his followers to summon the great day by dancing in a circle.

Until that time of deliverance, Wovoka insisted, Indians should live in peace with one another and with whites. He believed that whites would be destroyed in the apocalypse, however, and as the new Ghost Dance spread from tribe to tribe across the West, some Indians languishing on reservations saw the prophecy as divine retribution for their sufferings. Word of Wovoka's vision reached all the way to South Dakota, where disaffected Lakota Sioux practiced their own version of the Ghost Dance and predicted that whites would soon vanish from the face of the earth. Federal officials felt threatened by their fervor and launched an effort to suppress the

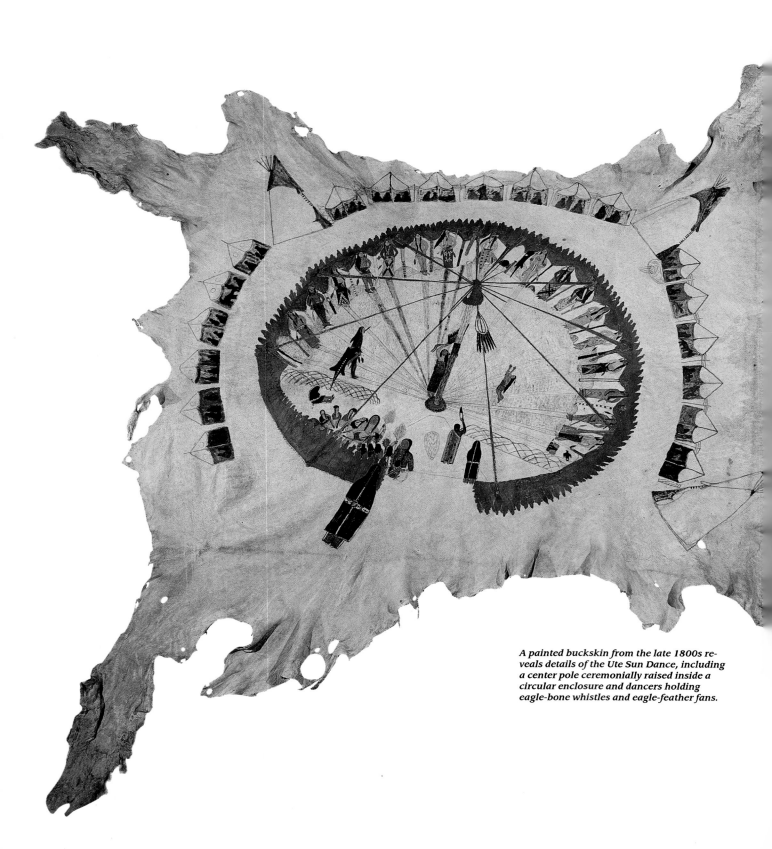

A painted buckskin from the late 1800s reveals details of the Ute Sun Dance, including a center pole ceremonially raised inside a circular enclosure and dancers holding eagle-bone whistles and eagle-feather fans.

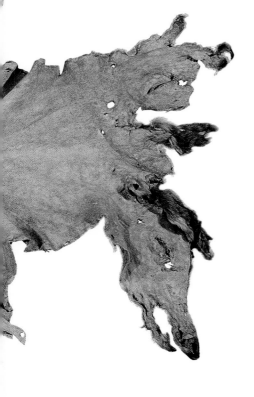

ritual that ended disastrously in December 1890 with the massacre at Wounded Knee of at least 200 Lakotas, mostly women and children.

Elsewhere, the Ghost Dance assumed a far different character. Eastern Shoshones and Utes derived a version of the rite that substituted the promise of good health for Wovoka's apocalypse. Participants wore blankets and shook them at the end of each dance in order to rid themselves of harmful ghosts and thus ensure good health. The ritual spread to other tribal groups around the Basin and continued to be performed long after Wovoka died in 1932, still a respected shaman but no longer a prophet of deliverance for Indians.

In addition to these homegrown ceremonies, various rituals from tribes to the east were adopted by Indians of the western range toward the end of the 19th century. The Utes, for example, acquired the Sun Dance from tribes living on the Plains, where the dance had long been the centerpiece of ceremonial life but had recently declined because of suppression by Indian agents and the collapse of buffalo hunting—the pursuit around which it revolved. Among the Utes, however, the ritual took on a new meaning. They danced for three days and nights without food or water and sought visions of the creator, whom they asked for strength to endure the trials of reservation life.

The ancient quest for visions lay at the heart of another practice that spread across the Great Basin during this period—the peyote cult. Adherents relied not on physical deprivation to stimulate visions but on the hallucinogenic effects of peyote, which Indians saw as a gift from the spirits. Originating among native peoples in Mexico and subsequently taken up by Comanches and other tribes that had been relegated to Oklahoma reservations, the peyote cult reached the Utes and other groups of the eastern Great Basin in the 1890s. In contrast to the fervor and spectacle that characterized both the Ghost Dance and the Sun Dance, the peyote ritual was subdued, typically accompanied by only a small drum and rattle and marked by prayer and contemplation. The ritual took on an air of defiance, however, when various states banned the use of peyote. Those laws led Indians to organize the Native American Church in 1918 to give the cult legitimacy as a formal religion.

The persistence of native religious movements in the 20th century reflected the determination of Indians across the region to preserve their cultural identity. Despite the allotment program and other federal policies aimed at "detribalizing" Indians, reservation dwellers continued to cherish their unique tribal communities. Some revived their collective fortunes by exploiting oil, natural gas, or mineral deposits on their remaining territory. Other groups went to court to assert their right to lands and resources that had been taken from them under questionable circumstances. Claims filed through the courts and the U.S. Indian Claims Commission brought tribes of the region awards ranging up to $50 million. The most ambitious claim was that of the Western Shoshones, who refused to take the money awarded by the government: They wanted nothing less than their old lands, covering more than one-third of Nevada.

The Western Shoshones asserted that they never had given up title to those lands. At issue was the Ruby Valley Treaty of 1863, negotiated between the United States and a dozen Western Shoshone leaders. In return for annual payments of $5,000 for 20 years, the chiefs agreed to the establishment of mines, ranches, railroads, and other enclaves within their territory. The federal government used those concessions as a pretext for taking over the entire tribal homeland with the exception of a few small Western Shoshone reserves, or farms. Some of the land acquired was sold or given away, while the rest became part of the public domain.

After long disputing the government's title to the territory, members of the tribe initiated a bold legal challenge in 1974. Two Western Shoshone sisters, Carrie and Mary Dann, were herding cattle on public rangeland near their 180-acre ranch in northeastern Nevada when an officer from the U.S. Bureau of Land Management approached them and asked to see their grazing permit. The Danns replied that they did not have one—and did not require one because the land belonged to the Western Shoshones. Their refusal to seek a permit was subsequently backed in court by the Sacred Lands Association, an organization that the Danns helped found for Western Shoshones who continued to believe "that Mother Earth is sacred and cannot be sold or destroyed."

Although the Indian Claims Commission tried to lay the issue to rest in 1979 by awarding the Western Shoshones $26 million for the lands taken from them by the government, the tribe voted to reject the award, and the Danns pressed their case in the federal courts. In 1985, however, the U.S. Supreme Court ruled that the Indian Claims Commission had extinguished the Shoshones' title to the land by setting aside in an account for the tribe the money it had elected to refuse. Western Shoshones, discouraged but still convinced of the validity of their claim, continued to argue their case in Congress and other forums.

Perhaps no group in the Great Basin fought longer or harder to preserve what remained of their inheritance than another Nevada group—the

Northern Paiutes living in the vicinity of Pyramid Lake. Three years after Chief Numaga died there in 1871, the area had finally been proclaimed an official reservation, but as it turned out, that decree did nothing to protect the waters the Paiutes depended on. In 1905 the federal government built a dam on the Truckee River that diverted about half the river's flow to irrigate farms and ranches located in northwestern Nevada. The diversion lowered the level of Pyramid Lake, significantly reducing its area and endangering the fish that afforded the resident Paiutes both sustenance and income. The water became increasingly alkaline, and a delta that formed at the mouth of the river prevented the fish from swimming upstream to spawn. By 1943 the cutthroat trout that the explorer Frémont had pronounced the best he ever tasted had to be restocked annually, and the cui-ui were in grave peril. With the fisheries virtually destroyed and the lake seemingly doomed, the reservation lost about two-thirds of its 1,500 residents.

Once again the Paiutes fought back. They asked the courts to uphold their right to receive enough of the Truckee River's flow to sustain healthy fisheries. Their legal challenge, like that of the Western Shoshones, failed on a technicality in the U.S. Supreme Court. But they found allies in environmentalists who joined with them in an effective political campaign that reduced diversions from the Truckee River and funded the construction of ladders, or spillways, for spawning fish. In 1990 an act of Congress ensured that the lake would continue to receive the water it needed to support life in abundance. Perhaps for the first time since white men set foot in the region, the Paiutes of Pyramid Lake could feel confident about the future of the precious desert refuge that nurtured the hopes of their ancestors and the dreams of their descendants. ◆

Releasing a rush of water and fish from a truck-borne tank, a Paiute woman dumps cutthroat trout back into Pyramid Lake after removing them temporarily for spawning. Paiutes have revived the lake's fisheries, once nearly wiped out by water diversions.

A RUGGED RACE FOR HONOR

Contestants in the annual race hold their mounts as they quietly contemplate the perilous slope of Suicide Hill. The racecourse is a daunting prospect for any rider.

From the time that horses first appeared on the Plateau, Indians there have relished the challenge of the race. The Indians' passion for horse racing endured despite confinement to reservations and the confiscation of their once thriving herds. During times of gathering, such as salmon days or first root harvest, men brought along their best horses and competed for prizes and honor.

The racing tradition lives on in the world-famous Suicide Race held near the Colville Confederated Tribes Indian Reservation in northern Washington State. Every August, Indians from all over the Plateau gather in tipi encampments to see old friends, participate in traditional dance contests, gamble in Indian stick games, and most important, to run the Suicide Race.

The short racecourse demands the most in skill and courage from both horse and rider. From the starting line, a short, flat straightaway provides just enough room for a horse to accelerate to full speed before hitting the crest of Suicide Hill, a screaming 210-foot drop that ends abruptly at the Okanogan River. Contestants must then cross almost 350 feet of swiftly moving water, climb the opposite bank, and then sprint to the finish line, just 980 feet from the starting line. The winner garners rewards and the adulation of the reservation children.

Since 1935 the race has been affiliated with the Omak Stampede, a rodeo sponsored by the town of Omak, Washington. Although it is still very much a traditional Indian race unfettered by restrictions, rigorous safety standards have been imposed to protect the riders and their mounts from serious injury. Riders must wear flotation vests and horses must be checked out by race veterinarians before they can even practice on the hair-raising course. Once the race begins, however, anything goes. Bumping, crowding, hitting, and even falling are all taken for granted. "When you're on that line, there's no more rules," explained a recent winner. "It's a free-for-all. If you can't handle it, you shouldn't be on the hill."

Contestants and their mounts plunge over the crest of Suicide Hill at full speed. Generations of men from the Colville Reservation have tested their mettle on the treacherous 33-degree slope.

Riders struggle for balance and position as their horses fight for footing on the hill's sandy terrain. Horse and rider must train diligently throughout the year to prepare for the run. Practice is critical because, says one race veteran, "You depend on your horse as much as you do yourself."

The lead horse crashes into the Okanogan
River as another mount spills its
rider farther up the hill. Although mishaps
such as this are frequent and
spectacular, serious injury is rare.

A safety boat rescues an unseated rider as his horse joins the other racers in the struggle to cross the Okanogan. Jockeys use their quirts to slap the water on either side of their horse's head to keep the animal focused and moving straight ahead.

Nearly 10,000 spectators watch as racers emerge from the river and thunder toward the finish line inside the rodeo arena. Race winners claim prize money, a new saddle, and a proud place among a people whose sporting tradition predates the written record books.

ACKNOWLEDGMENTS

The editors wish to thank the following individuals and institutions for their valuable assistance in the preparation of this volume:

In Canada:
Quebec—Robert Toupin, S.J., Institut Montserrat, Saint Jérôme.

In the United States:
Colorado: Denver—Rebecca Lintz, Colorado His-torical Society.

Idaho: Boise—Elizabeth Jacox, Idaho State His-torical Museum. Kamiah—Carla HighEagle, Nez Percé Appaloosa Horse Club. Moscow—Sue Emory, Appaloosa Museum and Heritage Center.

Oregon: Portland—Mikki Tint, Oregon Historical Society.

Nevada: Reno—Elmer Rusco; Kathryn Totton, University of Nevada Library.

Washington, D.C.—Felicia Pickering, Department of Anthropology, Vyrtis Thomas, National Anthro-pological Archives, Smithsonian Institution;

Thomas Rochford, S.J., National Jesuit Conference.

Washington State: Issaquah—Steven and Patricia Honnen. Seattle—Rebecca Andrews, Bill Holm, Robin K. Wright, The Thomas Burke Memorial Washington State Museum; Eugene Hunn, Sari Ott, Stan Shockey, University of Washington; Richard H. Engeman, Sandra Kroupa, John Medlin, Gary L. Menges, Carla Rickerson, Univer-sity of Washington Libraries. Tacoma—Elaine Miller, Joy Werlink, Washington State Historical Society. Vancouver—Jacqueline Peterson, Wash-ington State University.

BIBLIOGRAPHY

BOOKS

Aberle, David F., and Omer C. Stewart. *Peyotism in the West.* Salt Lake City: University of Utah Press, 1984.

Alter, J. Cecil, ed. *Jim Bridger.* Norman: University of Oklahoma Press, 1950.

America's Fascinating Indian Heritage. Pleasantville, N.Y.: Reader's Digest Association, 1978.

Andrews, Ralph W. *Curtis' Western Indians.* New York: Bonanza Books, 1962.

Axelrod, Alan. *Chronicle of the Indian Wars: From Colonial Times to Wounded Knee.* New York: Pren-tice Hall, 1993.

Blumberg, Rhoda. *The Incredible Journey of Lewis and Clark.* New York: Lothrop, Lee & Shepard, 1987.

Bolton, Herbert E. *Pageant in the Wilderness: The Story of the Escalante Expedition to the Interior Basin, 1776.* Salt Lake City: Utah State Historical Society, 1950.

Burt, Nathaniel. *Wyoming.* Oakland: Compass American Guides, 1991.

Canada's Native Peoples. Vol. 2 of *Canada Heirloom Series.* Mississauga, Ont.: Heirloom Publishing, 1988.

Canfield, Gae Whitney. *Sarah Winnemucca of the Northern Paiutes.* Norman: University of Okla-homa Press, 1983.

Capps, Benjamin, and the Editors of Time-Life Books. *The Great Chiefs* (The Old West series). Alexandria, Va.: Time Life Books, 1975.

Chittenden, Hiram Martin, and Alfred Talbot Richardson. *Life, Letters and Travels of Father Pierre-Jean De Smet, S.J.: 1801-1873.* 4 vols. New York: Francis P. Harper, 1905.

Clark, Ella E., and Margot Edmonds. *Sacagawea of the Lewis and Clark Expedition.* Los Angeles: Uni-versity of California Press, 1979.

Clokey, Richard M. *William H. Ashley: Enterprise and Politics in the Trans-Mississippi West.* Norman: University of Oklahoma Press, 1980.

Coe, Michael, Dean Snow, and Elizabeth Benson. *Atlas of Ancient America.* Oxford: Equinox, 1986.

Conetah, Fred A. *A History of the Northern Ute Peo-ple.* Edited by Katherine L. McKay and Floyd A. O'Neil. Salt Lake City: Uintah-Ouray Ute Tribe, 1982.

Conn, Richard. *Native American Art in the Denver Art Museum.* Denver: Denver Art Museum, 1979.

D'Azevedo, Warren L., ed. *Great Basin.* Vol. 11 of *Handbook of North American Indians.* Washing-ton, D.C.: Smithsonian Institution, 1986.

Delaney, Robert W. *The Ute Mountain Utes.* Albu-querque: University of New Mexico Press, 1989.

Dillon, Richard H. *North American Indian Wars.* New York: Gallery Books, 1983.

Donnelly, Joseph P., trans. *Wilderness Kingdom: Indi-an Life in the Rocky Mountains, 1840-1847, the Journals and Paintings of Nicolas Point, S.J.* New York: Holt, Rinehart and Winston, 1967.

Downs, James F. *The Two Worlds of the Washo: An Indian Tribe of California and Nevada.* New York: Holt, Rinehart and Winston, 1966.

Egan, Ferol. *Sand in a Worldwind: The Paiute Indian War of 1860.* Reno: University of Nevada Press, 1985.

Erdoes, Richard, and Alfonso Ortiz, eds. *American Indian Myths and Legends.* New York: Pantheon Books, 1984.

Ewers, John C.:
Artists of the Old West. Garden City, N.Y.: Double-day, 1965.
Gustavus Sohon's Portraits of Flathead and Pend D'Oreille Indians, 1854. Washington, D.C.: Smith-sonian Institution, 1948.
The Horse in Blackfoot Indian Culture: With Com-parative Material from Other Western Tribes. Washington, D.C.: Smithsonian Institution Press, 1955.

Ewers, John C., ed. *Adventures of Zenas Leonard, Fur Trader.* Norman: University of Oklahoma Press, 1959.

Ferris, Robert G., ed. *Lewis and Clark.* Washington, D.C.: U.S. Department of the Interior, 1975.

Fitz-Gerald, Christine A. *The World's Great Explorers: Meriwether Lewis and William Clark.* Chicago: Childrens Press, 1991.

Fleming, Paula Richardson, and Judith Luskey. *The North American Indians: In Early Photographs.* New York: Harper & Row, 1986.

Fowler, Catherine S.:
In the Shadow of Fox Peak: An Ethnography of the Cattail-Eater Northern Paiute People of Stillwater Marsh. Washington, D.C.: U.S. Department of the Interior, 1992.
"Settlement Patterns and Subsistence Systems in the Great Basin: The Ethnographic Record." In *Man and Environment in the Great Basin,* edited by David B. Madsen and James F. O'Con-nell. Washington, D.C.: Society for American Ar-chaeology, 1982.

Fowler, Don D. *The Western Photographs of John K. Hillers: Myself in the Water.* Washington, D.C.: Smithsonian Institution Press, 1989.

Franklin, Robert J., and Pamela A. Bunte. *The Paiute.* New York: Chelsea House Publishers, 1990.

Fremont, John Charles. *Narratives of Exploration and Adventure.* Edited by Allan Nevins. New York: Longmans, Green, 1956.

Gay, E. Jane. *With the Nez Perces: Alice Fletcher in the Field, 1889-92.* Lincoln: University of Nebraska Press, 1981.

Gilbert, Bil, and the Editors of Time-Life Books. *The Trailblazers* (The Old West series). Alexandria, Va.: Time Life Books, 1973.

Goodwin, Cardinal. *The Trans-Mississippi West: A History of Its Acquisition and Settlement.* New York: D. Appleton, 1922.

Gowans, Fred R. *Rocky Mountain Rendezvous.* Pro-vo, Utah: Brigham Young University Press, 1975.

Haddle, Jan. *The Complete Book of the Appaloosa.* New York: A. S. Barnes, 1975.

Haines, Francis. *Appaloosa: The Spotted Horse in Art and History.* Fort Worth: University of Texas Press, 1963.

Harris, Jack. "The White Knife Shoshoni of Nevada." In *Acculturation in Seven American Indian Tribes,* edited by Ralph Linton. Gloucester, Mass.: Peter Smith, 1963.

Hopkins, Sarah Winnemucca. *Life Among the Paiutes: Their Wrongs and Claims.* New York: G. P. Putnam and Sons, 1883.

Hultkrantz, Åke. *Belief and Worship in Native North America.* Edited by Christopher Vecsey. Syracuse, N.Y.: Syracuse University Press, 1981.

Janetski, Joel C. *The Indians of Yellowstone Park.* Salt Lake City: University of Utah Press, 1987.

Jennings, Jesse D., et al. *The Native Americans.* New York: Harper & Row, 1977.

Josephy, Alvin M. Jr. *The Nez Perce Indians and the Opening of the Northwest.* New Haven, Conn.: Yale University Press, 1965.

Knack, Martha C., and Omer C. Stewart. *As Long as the River Shall Run: An Ethnohistory of Pyramid Lake Indian Reservation.* Berkeley: University of California Press, 1984.

Kopper, Philip. *The Smithsonian Book of North Amer-ican Indians: Before the Coming of the Europeans.* Washington, D.C.: Smithsonian Books, 1986.

Lewis, Meriwether, and William Clark. *The History of the Lewis and Clark Expedition.* 3 vols. Edited by

Elliott Coues. New York: Dover Publications, 1994 (reprint of 1893 edition).

Life Stories of Our Native People: Shoshone, Paiute, Washo. Reno: Inter-Tribal Council of Nevada, 1974.

Madsen, Brigham D. *The Shoshoni Frontier: And the Bear River Massacre.* Salt Lake City: University of Utah Press, 1985.

Madsen, David B., and James F. O'Connell, eds. *Man and Environment in the Great Basin.* Washington, D.C.: Society for American Archaeology, 1982.

Miller, Christopher L. *Prophetic Worlds: Indians and Whites on the Columbia Plateau.* New Brunswick, N.J.: Rutgers University Press, 1985.

Morgan, Dale L. *Jedediah Smith and the Opening of the West.* Lincoln: University of Nebraska Press, 1953.

Mourning Dove. *Mourning Dove: A Salishan Autobiography.* Lincoln: University of Nebraska Press, 1990.

Murdock, G. P., and T. O'Leary. *Ethnographic Bibliography of North America.* Vol. 3. New Haven, Conn.: Human Relations Area Files Press, 1975.

Nicandri, David L. *Northwest Chiefs: Gustav Sohon's Views of the 1855 Stevens Treaty Councils.* Tacoma: Washington State Historical Society, 1986.

Numa: A Northern Paiute History. Reno: Inter-Tribal Council of Nevada, 1976.

Ogden, Peter Skene. *Snake Country Journal.* London: Hudson Bay Record Society, 1961.

Opler, Marvin K. "The Southern Ute of Colorado." In *Acculturation in Seven American Indian Tribes,* edited by Ralph Linton. Gloucester, Mass.: Peter Smith, 1963.

Patent, Dorothy Hinshaw. *Appaloosa Horses.* New York: Holiday House, 1988.

Peterson, Jacqueline. *Sacred Encounters: Father De Smet and the Indians of the Rocky Mountain West.* Norman: University of Oklahoma Press, 1993.

Ray, Verne F. *Cultural Relations in the Plateau of Northwestern America.* Los Angeles: Southwest Museum, 1939.

Ronda, James P. *Lewis and Clark among the Indians.* Lincoln: University of Nebraska Press, 1984.

Ross, Alexander. *Adventures of the First Settlers on the Columbia River.* Ann Arbor, Mich.: University Microfilms, 1966.

Ruby, Robert H., and John A. Brown:
Dreamer-Prophets of the Columbia Plateau: Smohalla and Skolaskin. Norman: University of Oklahoma Press, 1989.
The Spokane Indians: Children of the Sun. Norman: University of Oklahoma Press, 1970.

Scordato, Ellen. *Sarah Winnemucca: Northern Paiute Writer and Diplomat.* New York: Chelsea House Publishers, 1992.

Scott, Lalla. *Karnee: A Paiute Narrative.* Reno: University of Nevada Press, 1966.

Sherman, Josepha. *Indian Tribes of North America.* New York: Portland House, 1990.

Siskin, Edgar E. *Washo Shamans and Peyotists: Religious Conflict in an American Indian Tribe.* Salt Lake City: University of Utah Press, 1983.

Smith, Anne M., ed. *Shoshone Tales.* Salt Lake City: University of Utah Press, 1993.

Snow, Dean R. *The Archaeology of North America.* New York: Chelsea House Publishers, 1989.

Spencer, Robert F., and Jesse D. Jennings. *The Native Americans.* New York: Harper & Row, 1977.

Sprague, Marshall. *Massacre: The Tragedy at White River.* Boston: Little, Brown, 1957.

Steward, Julian H. *Basin-Plateau Aboriginal Sociopolitical Groups.* Washington, D.C.: U.S. Government Printing Office, 1938.

Stewart, Omer C. *Indians of the Great Basin: A Critical Bibliography.* Bloomington: Indiana University Press, 1982.

Story of the Great American West. Pleasantville, N.Y.: Reader's Digest Association, 1977.

Trenholm, Virginia Cole, and Maurine Carley. *The Shoshonis: Sentinels of the Rockies.* Norman: University of Oklahoma Press, 1964.

Turney-High, Harry Holbert. *The Flathead Indians of Montana.* Menasha, Wis.: American Anthropological Association, 1937.

Utley, Robert M.:
Frontier Regulars: The United States Army and the Indian, 1866-1891. New York: Macmillan, 1973.
Frontiersmen in Blue: The United States Army and the Indian, 1848-1865. New York: Macmillan, 1967.

Vecsey, Christopher, and Robert W. Venables, eds. *American Indian Environments: Ecological Issues in Native American History.* Syracuse, N.Y.: Syracuse University Press, 1980.

Waldman, Carl:
Atlas of the North American Indian. New York: Facts On File Publications, 1985.
Encyclopedia of Native American Tribes. New York: Facts On File Publications, 1988.

Walker, Deward E. Jr.:
Conflict and Schism in Nez Perce Acculturation: A Study of Religion and Politics. Moscow: University Press of Idaho, 1985.
Indians of Idaho. Moscow: University Press of Idaho, 1978.
Myths of Idaho Indians. Moscow: University Press of Idaho, 1980.

Walker, Deward E. Jr., ed. *Witchcraft and Sorcery of the American Native Peoples.* Moscow: University Press of Idaho, 1989.

Washburn, Wilcomb E., ed. *History of Indian-White Relations.* Vol. 4 of *Handbook of North American Indians.* Washington, D.C.: Smithsonian Institution, 1988.

The West of Alfred Jacob Miller: 1837. Norman: University of Oklahoma Press, 1968.

Westward on the Oregon Trail. New York: American Heritage Publishing, 1962.

Wheat, Margaret M. *Survival Arts of the Primitive Paiutes.* Reno: University of Nevada Press, 1967.

White, Richard. *"It's Your Misfortune and None of My Own": A History of the American West.* Norman: University of Oklahoma Press, 1991.

Wilfong, Cheryl. *Following the Nez Perce Trail: A Guide to the Nee-Me-Poo National Historic Trail with Eyewitness Accounts.* Corvallis: Oregon State University Press, 1990.

Williams, Chuck. *Bridge of the Gods, Mountains of Fire: A Return to the Columbia Gorge.* White Salmon, Wash., and New York: Elephant Mountain Arts and Friends of the Earth, 1980.

Wood, Nancy. *When Buffalo Free the Mountains.* Garden City, N.Y.: Doubleday, 1980.

Wright, Robin K., ed. *A Time of Gathering: Native Heritage in Washington State.* Seattle: Burke Museum and University of Washington Press, 1991.

PERIODICALS

Anderson, Irving W. "Probing the Riddle of the Bird Woman." *Montana: The Magazine of Western History,* Fall 1973.

Austin, Carol. "Home Again." *Equus,* September 1993.

Bennett, Deb. "The Origin of Horse Breeds: What 'Flavor' Is Your Horse?" *Equus,* March 1987.

Brooks, Juanita. "Indian Relations on the Mormon Frontier." *Utah State Historical Society,* January-April 1944.

Dawson, Robert, and Peter Goin. "Pyramid Lake Project." *Nevada Public Affairs Review,* 1992.

"Gambling on Indian Reservations." *Editorial Research Reports,* November 9, 1990.

Hendrick, Kimmis:
"Indians Gain Backing in Battle to Save Pyramid Lake." *The Christian Science Monitor,* May 5, 1969.
"Nevada's 'Gem in the Mountains' Dispute." *The Christian Science Monitor,* September 3, 1970.
"Paiute Indians Fight to Keep Lake." *The Christian Science Monitor,* May 27, 1968.

Hodge, Paul. "Nevada Tribe Wins Suit on Water Rights." *Washington Post,* November 10, 1972.

"The Indian Water Wars." *Newsweek,* June 13, 1983.

Peterson, Nella:
"What is an Appaloosa?" Part 1. *Appaloosa Journal,* October 1990.
"What is an Appaloosa?" Part 2. *Appaloosa Journal,* November 1990.
"What is an Appaloosa?" Part 3. *Appaloosa Journal,* December 1990.

Roberts, Steven V. "Nevada Indians Fight for a Lake." *The New York Times,* February 23, 1969.

Rusco, Elmer R.:
"Historical Change in Western Shoshone Country: The Establishment of the Western Shoshone National Council and Traditionalist Land Claims." *American Indian Quarterly,* Summer 1992.
"The Truckee-Carson-Pyramid Lake Water Rights Settlement Act and Pyramid Lake." *Nevada Public Affairs Review,* 1992.

Speth, Lembi Kongas. "Possible Fishing Cliques among the Northern Paiutes of the Walker River Reservation, Nevada." *Ethnohistory,* Summer 1969.

Sylvester, Kathleen. "Indians Bet on the Lure of the Dice." *Governing,* July 1993.

Wall, Kathleen. "Rekindled Spirits." *Appaloosa Journal,* June 1992.

Webb, Mary. "Pyramid Lake: The Tonic of Wilderness." *Nevada Public Affairs Review,* 1992.

Wexler, Mark. "Sacred Rights." *National Wildlife,* June-July 1992.

OTHER SOURCES

"Cornhusk Bags of the Plateau Indians." Catalog. Spokane: Cheney Cowles Museum, 1974.

"Cornhusk Bags of the Plateau Indians." Catalog. Springdale, Wash.: Maryhill Museum, n.d.

"Glass Tapestry." Catalog. Phoenix: The Heard Museum, November 1993.

Harrison, Lynn:
"Patriotic Symbols in American Indian Art." Catalog. Spokane: Cheney Cowles Museum, 1992.
"Traditions: Beadwork of the Native American." Spokane: Cheney Cowles Museum, n.d.

PICTURE CREDITS

The sources for the illustrations that appear in this book are listed below. Credits from left to right are separated by colons; from top to bottom they are separated by dashes.

Cover: Nella Peterson. **6, 7:** Background © Carr Clifton. National Anthropological Archives (NAA), Smithsonian Institution, neg. no. 42021-A; © David Stoecklein/The Stock Solution. **8, 9:** Background © Carr Clifton. Cheney Cowles Museum; Sharon Eva Grainger. **10, 11:** Background © Carr Clifton. Latter Day Saints Church Archives, Salt Lake City, Utah; © Stephen Trimble. **12, 13:** Background © Carr Clifton. Library of Congress; © Randy Kalisek/F-Stock, Inc. **14, 15:** Background © Carr Clifton. Library of Congress; Kenneth L. Miller. **16:** Field Museum, Chicago, neg. no. A29TC; The Walters Art Gallery, Baltimore. **18, 19:** © Carr Clifton. **20:** © 1990 Ed Castle/Michael Ventura Photography—Library of Congress. **21:** © 1990 Ed Castle/Michael Ventura Photography. **22:** Map by Maryland CartoGraphics, Inc. **23:** College of Eastern Utah Prehistoric Museum, Price, Utah, photo: Pearl Oliver. **24, 25:** © Carr Clifton—NAA, Smithsonian Institution, neg. no. 1712-B. **26, 27:** © Steve Bly/F-Stock, Inc.—© David Stoecklein/F-Stock, Inc. **28, 29:** Courtesy Mary DiSilvestre. **30:** The Honnen Collection; © 1994 Eduardo Calderón, The Honnen Collection (3)—private collection, Belgium, courtesy The De Smet Project, Washington State Univ. **33:** Missouri Historical Society. **34, 35:** Oregon Historical Society, neg. no. 45452; Library of Congress. **36:** Cheney Cowles Museum. **37:** Library of Congress. **38:** Thomas Rochford, S.J., National Jesuit News, Washington, D.C.; Washington State Historical Society; Nez Percé National Historical Park, Spalding, Ida., courtesy The De Smet Project, Washington State Univ. **39:** Courtesy Thomas Burke Memorial Washington State Museum, photo by Eugene Hunn. **40, 41:** Nevada Historical Society. **42:** Library of Congress. **45:** Oregon Historical Society, neg. no. 4466-A. **46:** Denver Art Museum, acq. no. 1964.156, photographed by Lloyd Rule; Library of Congress. **49:** Cheney Cowles Museum; Cheney Cowles Museum, courtesy The De Smet Project, Washington State Univ. **50, 51:** Cheney Cowles Museum—Historical Photograph Collections, Washington State Univ. Libraries, neg. no. 77-022; Cheney Cowles Museum (4). **52:** Western History Collections, Univ. of Oklahoma Library. **53:** Flathead Cultural Commission, St. Ignatius, Mont., courtesy The De Smet Project, Washington State Univ. **55:** Glenbow Archives, Calgary, Alta., photo. no. NA-1431-28. **56, 57:** © Stephen Trimble; courtesy Colorado Historical Society, Ute Museum. **58:** Library of Congress, USZ-62-12318-N. **59:** Special Collections Dept., Univ. of Nevada, Reno Library, Margaret M. Wheat Collection, photo. no. P89-32/17. **60:** NAA, Smithsonian Institution, neg. no. 72-613—Scott W. Klette, Nevada State Museum, Carson City, Nev. **61:** Scott W. Klette, Nevada State Museum, Carson City, Nev.—Special Collections Dept., Univ. of Nevada, Reno Library, Margaret M. Wheat Collection, photo. no. P89-32/95. **62, 63:** Special Collections Dept., Univ. of Nevada, Reno Library, photo. no. P89-32/43—Scott W. Klette, Nevada State Museum, Carson City,

Nev.—Special Collections Dept., Univ. of Nevada, Reno Library, Margaret M. Wheat Collection, photo. no. P89-32/77, P89-32/67; photo by Don Eiler, courtesy Dept. of Library Services, American Museum of Natural History. **64:** Special Collections Dept., Univ. of Nevada, Reno Library, Gus Bundy Collection, photo. no. P85-08/37183; C. Chesek, American Museum of Natural History. **65:** Special Collections Dept., Univ. of Nevada, Reno Library, Margaret M. Wheat Collection, photo. no. P89-32/111—NAA, Smithsonian Institution, no. 94-12252. **66:** NAA, Smithsonian Institution, neg. no. 1607—Scott W. Klette, Nevada State Museum, Carson City, Nev. **67:** Nevada Historical Society—Special Collections Dept., Univ. of Nevada, Reno Library, Margaret M. Wheat Collection, photo. no. P89-32/30; Scott W. Klette, Nevada State Museum, Carson City, Nev. **68:** Special Collections Dept., Univ. of Nevada, Reno Library, Margaret M. Wheat Collection, photo. no. P89-32/99, P89-32/145. **69:** NAA, Smithsonian Institution, neg. no. 94-12251, 94-1623. **70, 71:** Peter Turnley/Black Star. **72, 73:** Copyright British Museum, London; copyright British Library, London—courtesy The Bancroft Library, Univ. of California, Berkeley. **74, 75:** Ernst Haas; Thomas Gilcrease Institute of American History and Art—map by Maryland CartoGraphics, Inc. **76, 77:** Courtesy Thomas Burke Memorial Washington State Museum, catalog number 2-1537; The Appaloosa Museum and Heritage Center, Moscow, Ida.—NAA, Smithsonian Institution, neg. no. 2975-D-2. **78, 79:** Nella Peterson, courtesy The Nez Percé Appaloosa Horse Club. **80:** Thomas Rochford, S.J., courtesy Archives des Jesuites, St. Jérôme, Que. **83:** Courtesy Colorado Historical Society, W. H. Jackson Photo, neg. no. F8767. **84:** American Philosophical Society. **85:** New York Historical Society; Peabody Museum, Harvard Univ., photo by Hillel Burger. **86:** John Eastcott/YVA Momatiuk. **88, 89:** Map by Maryland CartoGraphics, Inc. **90:** Bibliothèque Nationale de France, Paris. **91:** Paulus Leeser, courtesy Art and Architecture Division, The New York Public Library, Astor, Lenox and Tilden Foundations. **92, 93:** © Carr Clifton. **96-98:** The Walters Art Gallery, Baltimore. **100:** Field Museum, Chicago, courtesy The De Smet Project, Washington State Univ. **102, 103:** National Museum of American Art, Washington, D.C./Art Resource, N.Y. (2); Oregon Historical Society, neg. no. OrHi #637. **104, 105:** National Park Service, Nez Percé National Historical Park, Mrs. Richard Klason Collection, neg. no. 0589; Idaho State Historical Society, neg. no. 63-221.882. **106:** Jozef Dauwe, Lebbeke, Belgium, courtesy The De Smet Project, Washington State Univ. **107:** Oregon Historical Society, neg. no. OrHi #87847. **108, 109:** Thomas Rochford, S.J., courtesy De Smetiana Collection, Jesuit Missouri Province Archives, St. Louis—Jesuit Missouri Province Archives, St. Louis, courtesy The De Smet Project, Washington State Univ. **110:** Jesuit Missouri Province Archives, St. Louis, courtesy The De Smet Project, Washington State Univ. **112, 113:** Courtesy Thomas Burke Memorial Washington State Museum, property of The Honnen Collection; Field Museum, Chicago, courtesy The De Smet Project, Washington State Univ.; Peabody Museum, Harvard Univ., photo by Hillel Burger. **115:** Photo courtesy Latter Day Saints Church Archives, Salt Lake City, Utah. **117:** NAA,

Smithsonian Institution, neg. no. 1663-A. **118:** Nevada Historical Society. **120:** Thomas Rochford, S.J., courtesy Archives des Jesuites, St. Jérôme, Que. **121:** Brian Merrett, Montreal, courtesy Archives des Jesuites, St. Jérôme, Que. **122:** Thomas Rochford, S.J., courtesy Archives des Jesuites, St. Jérôme, Que. **123:** Jesuit Missouri Province Archives, St. Louis, courtesy The De Smet Project, Washington State Univ.—Thomas Rochford, S.J., courtesy Archives des Jesuites, St. Jérôme, Que. (3). **124:** Thomas Rochford, S.J., courtesy Archives des Jesuites, St. Jérôme, Que. (2)—Brian Merrett, Montreal, courtesy Archives des Jesuites, St. Jérôme, Que. **125:** Thomas Rochford, S.J., courtesy Archives des Jesuites, St. Jérôme, Que.—Jesuit Missouri Province Archives, St. Louis, courtesy The De Smet Project, Washington State Univ. **126:** Brian Merrett, Montreal, courtesy Archives des Jesuites, St. Jérôme, Que.—Thomas Rochford, S.J., courtesy Archives des Jesuites, St. Jérôme, Que. **127:** Thomas Rochford, S.J., courtesy Archives des Jesuites, St. Jérôme, Que.—Jesuit Missouri Province Archives, St. Louis, courtesy The De Smet Project, Washington State Univ. **128:** Thomas Rochford, S.J., courtesy De Smetiana Collection, Jesuit Missouri Province Archives, St. Louis. **129:** Thomas Rochford, S.J., courtesy Archives des Jesuites, St. Jérôme, Que. **130:** Brian Merrett, Montreal, courtesy Archives des Jesuites, St. Jérôme, Que. **131:** Jesuit Missouri Province Archives, St. Louis, courtesy The De Smet Project, Washington State Univ.—Thomas Rochford, S.J., courtesy Archives des Jesuites, St. Jérôme, Que. **132:** Courtesy Colorado Historical Society, Ute Museum, trans. no. F7051. **134, 135:** Kenneth L. Miller. **136:** Nevada Historical Society. **137:** Special Collections Dept., Univ. of Nevada, Reno Library, photo. no. 156. **138:** Courtesy Colorado Historical Society, Ute Museum. **139:** NAA, Smithsonian Institution, neg. no. 1613-A-1. **140:** Nevada Historical Society. **141:** California Historical Society; Special Collections Dept., Univ. of Nevada, Reno Library, photo. no. 217/A. **142:** The Bancroft Library, Univ. of California, Berkeley. **144:** Washington State Historical Society. **145:** Denver Public Library, Western History Dept., neg. no. F47232—Washington State Historical Society. **146, 147:** Washington State Historical Society. **148, 149:** Library of Congress, USZ-62-47006. **150:** NAA, Smithsonian Institution, neg. no. 45744. **151:** Washington State Historical Society. **152, 153:** NAA, Smithsonian Institution, neg. no. 2976, 2906; Dr. Norris H. Perkins. **154:** © 1994 George White Jr. **156, 157:** NAA, Smithsonian Institution, neg. no. 1535. **158:** Montrose County Historical Museum. **159:** Courtesy Colorado Historical Society, Ute Museum. **160, 161:** Courtesy Colorado Historical Society, Ute Museum, trans. no. 81-195.52 A—Missouri Historical Society; courtesy Colorado Historical Society, Ute Museum, F31, 1801F. **162:** Missouri Historical Society; courtesy Colorado Historical Society, Ute Museum. **164, 165:** Montana Historical Society; Mansfield Library, Univ. of Montana. **166, 167:** Oregon Historical Society, neg. no. GI #8307; courtesy Colorado Historical Society, Ute Museum (2). **168, 169:** NAA, Smithsonian Institution, neg. no. 2903A. **170, 171:** Colorado Historical Society, Ute Museum, trans. no. E.1894.171. **172:** Kenneth L. Miller. **174-185:** Sharon Eva Grainger.

INDEX

Numerals in italics indicate an illustration of the subject mentioned.